CYCLING ALONG THE WATERWAYS OF FRANCE

Tony Roberts

BICYCLE  BOOKS

FROM

MBI Publishing Company

First published in 1998 by MBI Publishing Company, 729 Prospect Avenue, PO Box 1, Osceola, WI 54020-0001 USA

MBI Publishing Company books are also available at discounts in bulk quantity for industrial or sales-promotional use. For details write to Special Sales Manager at Motorbooks International Wholesalers & Distributors, 729 Prospect Avenue, PO Box 1, Osceola, WI 54020-0001 USA

Library of Congress Cataloging-in-Publication Data
        Roberts, Tony.
        Cycling along the waterways of France/Tony Roberts.
            p. cm.--(Bicycle books)
        Includes index.
        ISBN 0-933201-90-7 (pbk.: alk. paper)
1. Cycling--France--Guidebooks. 2.
Waterways--France--Guidebooks.
3. France--Guidebooks. I. Title. II. Series.
GV1046.F8R63   1998
914.404'839--dc21   98-10282

On the front cover: The beautiful canals of France lend themselves perfectly to scenic cycling.

On the back cover: Gravel and brick towpaths line the canals and make a reasonable surface for cycling throughout France.

Printed in the United States of America

Contents

Note

Nothing can ruin a good day of cycling faster than having your progress halted by the termination of the path you are following. Or the expectations of a hotel around the bend that is no longer in business.

In advance, we offer our deepest apologies. We need not be prescient to know that changes happen. Floods can destroy a towpath, hotels go out of business, and a restaurant that was superb last year may be a disaster today.

Each turn of the recommended routes has been personally checked by the author. But changes are a way of life. The path that existed yesterday on the right bank may today exist on the left—or not exist at all.

We're sorry, but it happens.

You can help. Please set us and future editions to rights by writing your comments, updates, and corrections to the publisher. Those who follow in your wheel tracks will thank you, too.

On a recent trip to France I called at the office of the French bicycle touring association, the *Fédération Française de Cyclotourisme,* to discuss my book idea with the executives.

"Oh, Monsieur, yes, it is indeed possible to ride long distances along the canal towpaths," I was told, "but you must understand that the government has not yet endorsed this and you will do it at your own risk."

I let this statement sink in a minute. "But, Monsieur," I responded in my best French, "aren't I in far greater risk riding on the shoulder of a highway filled with speeding French drivers?"

My friend just shrugged his shoulders Gallicly.

Tony Roberts
Sisters, Oregon

PART I

Preface

One morning while I was piloting my sailing vessel from the North Sea to the Mediterranean via the extensive French system of interconnected canals and rivers, I found myself on a peaceful backcountry canal in Burgundy. My boat was tied to a tree along the bank where I had spent a quiet night. Paralleling and not far away was a busy two-lane highway on which was moving a substantial amount of traffic—speeding cars, smoking 18-wheelers, and, trying hard to keep out of their way, a number of cycling tourists—in the argot of the long-distance biker, white-liners. France, I remembered, is a prime international tourist destination, and doing it by bicycle a long-time favorite way to experience it.

My observations of the highway parade were interrupted by the approach of two French housewives. The ladies were riding ancient single-speed bicycles, not on the highway but along the old canal towpath, and would pass within a few feet of me. A happy infant was peeking out of one lady's front pack. Both bicycles had sturdy wooden fruit boxes lashed to rear carriers, and each was heavy-laden with market purchases.

The ladies moved past me, seemingly effortlessly. Their animated chatter was interrupted by my greeting and their response, "Bonjour, Monsieur." The gravel surface of the path was smooth and, of course, as absolutely level as the surface of the canal it ran beside. It was the beginning of what promised to be a hot summer day, but their route was cool, wonderfully shaded by the long line of poplar trees that stretched off into the haze in both directions.

I could see by the swaying of the high branches of the poplars that the breeze had already started. But the canal was in the bottom of a cut where the breeze neither ruffled the water nor impeded the ladies' progress.

Cyclists will see lots of people fishing along the routes. It's a common activity, but there is seldom much sign of success.

I reflected on an enigma. Why, I wondered, would cyclists suffer the tumultuous racket, the blasts of noxious fumes, and the very real hazards of the highway, rushing by only inches from their elbows, when this quiet option was so near?

Part of the answer, of course, is that there are more highways than there are canal paths. They tend to be habit-forming. Another part of the answer may be that those who chose the highway didn't know any better and weren't as knowledgeable as the two local ladies.

It's probable the ladies had used the quiet canal route every market day for years, as did their mothers and grandmothers before them. My guess is they never even consider the highway. For one thing, how could they exchange the day's gossip over the ubiquitous traffic noises?

Join me as we cycle the towpaths through some of the most scenically beautiful, historically important, and culturally endowed areas of the world. Let's saddle up and leave our worries back with the traffic. But first, some background and a few pointers to make your travels more pleasant and hassle-free.

Prologue:
Canal Cycling—A New
and Different Philosophy

H illary climbed Mt. Everest because it was there, not because it was fun. To a large degree, cyclists, too, undertake grueling treks and battle mountains, deserts, the cyclonic winds of passing 18-wheelers, and the near misses of speeding vacationers for one principal reason: to conquer.

Smelling the roses has not been a part of the agenda. Perhaps the reason is simple: Cyclists are far too busy with the mile-by-mile need to keep out of harm's way. Perhaps, also, being a part of the frenetic pace of the highway and its denizens, in itself, discourages a slower, more rewarding pace.

But long distance bike touring doesn't have to be simply a rush to completion. It can be a peaceful Sunday ride through the park with your family, taken to the nth power. That is the essence of canal touring, the addition of peace and joy and learning to what was once solely the thrill of accomplishment.

You can still post your highlighted route map on your study wall. You can still say to your couch potato guests, "See, we did that."

But your rewards will go far beyond. Following the gravel paths, *les chemins d'halage*, of this long, skinny, almost-private park, provides an intimacy with the countryside you can never experience in highway biking or in a car, train, or airplane.

If it is the rushing pace of highway vehicles that breeds a relentless need to race for the finish, it may be the characteristic quietude of a canal bank that fosters, in the canal cyclist, the urge to slow down, to take a break from the pace that commands our everyday lives.

"Because it is there" should never be your prime motive. Substitute another motivation: "Because it is fascinating." Then take loads of time and let yourself be fascinated.

Towpath Touring—Some Reasons Why

No screeches, smells, or danger of traffic

Quiet backcountry lanes

You can take the whole family

Almost no hills to climb

Protected from the wind

Shaded from the sun

Close to nature, birds, animals

No broken glass to dodge, almost no roadside litter

No garish outdoor billboards

Time to observe the country, culture, and people.

Cyclists needn't be discouraged by barricades like this which apply to four-wheeled vehicles only.

Introduction:
The Enchantment of
Canalside Riding

"Every man has two countries, his own and France."
—Danton

P icture a gravel lane bordered on one side by a military line of poplars or plane trees and a gentle waterway on the other. Picture yourself aboard a reliable, responsive bike, happily following this friendly pathway along fertile valleys full of grain, sunflower fields, and sleeping cows, past historic old villages, through modern cities, alongside slumbering peasant farmhouses and opulent *châteaux* and through marshes full of ducks and moss and high reeds. This is the milieu of the "water roads" of France, and it is yours entirely without charge.

You are about to enjoy an unintended dividend to the inland waterway system of France, 5,300 miles of navigable rivers and man-made canals, the longest and most highly developed of its kind in the world. At its establishment, some as early as the sixteenth century, the carefully graded and graveled paths next to the waterways were as vital to the system as the water itself. Power for the early boats came from oxen, horses, and mules that traveled these paths pulling the barges behind them.

Today the animals have disappeared, but the towpaths, to a large degree, still exist and beckon cycling travelers eager to substitute a peaceful environment for the increasing turmoil of the highways. How fortunate that these routes pass through some of the country's most picturesque and varied geography!

Today the commercial barge traffic has disappeared almost as totally as the draft animals, victim of the railroad, the truck, and the container. When commercial traffic fell off sharply about three decades ago, the economy ax started to fall, and a number of canals were simply abandoned, closed ostensibly forever. The entire canal system might have had the same fate had it not been for the increase in French disposable income, longer vacations, and the development of reliable small marine engines. Vacationing Frenchmen suddenly discovered the sport of canal boating.

At about the same time, with British firms in the forefront, the canals birthed a rapidly growing holiday rental boat business: cabin cruisers available by the day, week, or longer for leisurely water wandering. Even first-time sailors found they could pilot their families through France without the need for experience or credentials. At 5 miles per hour, the canal speed limit, even novice captains give insurance companies no problem.

At the same time yet another vacation idea came into vogue: the use of luxuriously converted commercial barges as traveling waterway hotels. Often pitching gastronomic as well as scenic adventure, these up-market offerings are common sights today along every waterway.

Just in the nick of time, the body count of boats passing through the system stopped its sharp downward trend and the numbers started back up. The bureaucrats took another look, and the canals got a reprieve, a national jewel to be preserved, no matter the cost.

In some places, notably the Canal du Midi, the canal has brought welcome new tourism to villages and towns once far off the beaten tourist path. Many have built marinas and port facilities, waterside parks, and tourist information offices to court the nautical, hiking, and cycling canalside passersby.

As this is written, canal towpaths exist in a wide range of conditions—from something that looks like a Tom Thumb edition of a trafficless San Diego Freeway to a single bumpy track through the tall grass. Usually, however, the path will be a happy compromise. Boat traffic has a direct effect upon towpath condition—the more traffic, the better the condition of the path. In the transition period between commercial and pleasure boating, the towpaths fared poorly, but many now are coming back.

Currently, with boating traffic increased by French vacationers and tourism, there is increased use of the paths. Boat crews use bikes and the paths for provisioning and for off-canal exploration. Villages looking to woo vacationers have also made towpath improvements to help merchants ring their tills. All of which has helped to bring the paths back.

Still, following the canal paths is not always as straightforward as you might think. At this writing, no single national authority has yet officially recognized their touristic potential. There is no standard for pathway maintenance, no organized set of signs to tell you which side to follow. Without the maps provided here, sometimes your path will, without warning, dead-end, forcing you to return to the last bridge and try the other side. Occasionally, paths on both sides will have disappeared, leaving no option but to use dead reckoning on local roads until you find the place where the canal path resumes. With this book, the reckoning has been done. The guesswork is removed, so you can keep going in a more or less straight line.

A curse of the touring cyclist is wind; just ask any fatigued traveler who has spent an afternoon working against a 25-knot headwind. Towpaths aren't free of this scourge, but far freer

Much of the routes are bordered by forests like this. Maintained meticulously, the trees are treated as a renewable crop.

than the open highway.

Thank the French custom of planting rows of trees along their waterways. These tree lines provide not only welcome shade to the cyclist, but also shelter from the wind. Often the canals lie in the bottom of an earth cut. This, too, minimizes wind exposure.

Without special authorization, automotive traffic is forbidden on canal paths. The few vehicles you encounter are driven by lockkeepers, canal maintenance crews, or occasional villagers traveling to their favorite trout pools.

Who else might you encounter along the way? Locals use the paths for exercising their dogs and for shopping or hiking excursions, the latter often in large groups. Holiday boat crews use them for the morning croissant run and to visit off-route points of interest. Lovers use the paths to get away from it all, as do equestrians and backpackers. Occasionally you encounter another intelligent touring cyclist. Near big cities like Toulouse, the path is filled morning and evening with well-dressed commuters whose briefcases are bungeed to their racks.

Often you'll hear shouts of greeting from the boats you pass. Most of them will be self-made Captain Hornblowers on rental boats, but some will be long-distance yachtsmen using the waterway system to travel between the English Channel and the Mediterranean. You can always spot the latter by their cluttered decks and salty demeanor. But mostly the canalside belongs to you—and the song birds, water fowl, and scurrying animals that inhabit the lovely water world the canals have made.

The canals are not used at night. The locks are shut down and the boatmen find places to tie up until morning. Often it is simply a convenient tree alongside the bank. They are forbidden to block the towpath with mooring lines, but be careful, as some don't get the word, and a garroting can ruin a good day.

French highways are becoming festooned with garish outdoor billboards, particularly dense and unsightly at the edge of cities and towns. Canalside cyclists are spared this ugliness. So far nobody has planted any ad signs along the canals. In contrast to highway cyclists, you often enter populated areas along paved, well-maintained pathways and through parks where ugliness is banned, one hopes forever.

The French are inveterate fishermen and, though normally law-abiding, if anyone is going to violate the ordinance that forbids cars on the towpath, it will be a local Waltonian for whom no *interdit* sign will impede his basic urge. You may have cycled alone for an hour or more along the canal bank with no evidence of humanity, when suddenly you come upon an ancient Deux Chevaux, and a man under a beret minding three or four rods.

Often the fisherman's attention to his bobbers is so intense he won't notice your approach. Greet him, but softly and be sure you don't run over his rods or his tackle box. Other path dangers to watch out for are unmarked sinkholes caused by water erosion. Watch out particularly alongside plane trees where, without warning, their aboveground roots may cause a wheel-bending disaster.

Make sure your pockets are secured before starting out. Valuable items have a habit of getting dislodged if the path is rough.

Locks

Called *écluses*, they are an omnipresent part of the canal system. They are major confrontations for boatmen, but no more than distractions and progress markers for cyclists. Along three canals, about 519 miles, there are 360 locks, an average of one lock each mile and a quarter. As a landsman, you simply cycle up or down a short, sharp hill corresponding to the height of the lock and pass alongside the lock gates. (Note: Some of the older lock mechanisms have long iron rods used as levers for working the gates. Be careful as you ride by, as the levers are at shoulder height.)

In the old days each lock was tended by a lockkeeper, an *éclusier*, who, with his family, lived alongside in a simple, government-issue, stone cottage. Economy moves have made major changes in some areas. As many as twenty or thirty locks may now be the responsibility of one lockkeeper, who often travels from one to the next along the path by motor bike. Some locks have been automated so that they can be operated electronically by the boatmen themselves. Along some canals, like the Canal de Bourgogne, many lockkeepers' houses have been abandoned or leased to vacationers.

Some locks are in metropolitan cities, some in villages, while others sit all alone in open countryside or forest glade. Where the canal engineers found the going steep, locks were built adjoining each other in groups or steps. In Brittany's Canal Nantes à Brest, within the first 10 miles from Pontivy, there are 53 locks in three separate stairways.

Lockkeepers spend a large amount of their time waiting for business. When they see a cyclist approaching, it may be a crewman sent ahead to alert him to have the gates open and the lock ready. Thus, when the lockkeeper looks at you with a questioning eye, shake your head "no" if no boat is approaching. The lockkeeper can then get back to his contemplation.

In areas where traffic still warrants one lockkeeper per lock, many have become entrepreneurs, offering local wine, fresh fruit, vegetables, and craft items to passersby. Often lockkeepers have beautified their surroundings with flower boxes, gardens, and well-kept lawns. One lockkeeper, obviously a music lover, has equipped himself with state-of-the-art audio equipment.

Don't be surprised to hear an amplified aria from Carmen as you pass by.

For cyclists the locks, each named and numbered, become easily identified mileposts. The same with bridges, tunnels, and aqueducts. Most bridges span both the path and the canal, so you can pass underneath without slowing. Sometimes, however, it's necessary to climb, cross the highway at grade, and ride down the other side to regain the path.

Where the canal intersects a stream or river, the engineers often constructed a bridge to carry it and its path over the intersecting waterway. On the Canal du Midi many of these aqueducts are original, more than 300 years old. They don't slow you down except where the rounded river stones are used as paving, although they will shake you up a bit if you're traveling at speed.

When mountains too big to lock over crossed their path, engineers tunneled through them. One, on the Canal de Bourgogne, is 2 miles long. Before the age of mechanization, barges went through by manual power or were winched through, so there is no towpath. Cyclists use back roads and reconnect with the canal where it emerges.

Randonnées

Canal path followers should not feel enslaved to the canal route. Thanks to an extensive national network of hiking trails, called *randonnées*, which often intersect with the canal path, you have a diversity of additional routes to explore, all equally free of highway traffic.

The trail network, which extends more than 25,000 miles in France, was organized by hiking clubs shortly after World War II. Famous routes include Grande Randonnée 65, which follows in a general way the ancient pilgrim route through France to St. Jacques de Compostelle in Spain. Another is the TMB, Tour de Mont Blanc, and the 600-mile GR 3, which transits the Loire Valley.

For each canal route covered here, an overall map shows the relationship of the canal to the *grande randonnées*. Cyclists are welcome to use these trails as long as they observe normal courtesy toward hikers and equestrians, and follow other basic rules.

Maintenance of the trails is the responsibility of local mayors or hiking clubs. Some will be in better condition than others. The path routes are chosen more for their scenic views and points of interest than for their directness.

For more information about *randonnées* in specific regions and for maps and guidebooks, write: La Fédération Française de Randonnée Pédestre, 8 Avenue Marceau, 75008 Paris.

Chapter 1

Planning Ahead— Things to Do Before You Leave

Half the fun of an adventure is in the anticipation and the planning. There's much thinking and organizing to do before you even leave your easy chair, so let's start having fun.

One of the first subjects to consider is your itinerary. How many or which of the canals do you want to explore? What other places to see, things to do, are on your mind? Remember, a large part of your investment is in the getting there. Once there, the additional cost for extra days, extra cities, extra activities is incidental.

For most people, time is more scarce than money, but if you are a first-time visitor to France, it would be a serious error to miss at least a weekend spent discovering Paris, the City of Light. If at all possible, put that on your itinerary.

The difference between a traveler and a tourist is that a traveler moves with a purpose, with intimacy. He tries to immerse himself in the culture, history, and scenery of the country he is visiting. Try to be a traveler, not a tourist. Are there special subjects that fascinate you? For example, if you're a gourmet cook, study up on the regional cooking of the area you'll be passing through, and sample the more exotic of its gastronomic offerings.

Maybe construction interests you. Get some books from your library on Romanesque, Medieval, and Renaissance architecture and learn how the ancients solved their structural problems. Examples of each epoch will be on every hand as you cycle through France.

How long will it take? To organize an itinerary it's necessary to be able to estimate how long it will take to complete your cycling route or routes. If you are a noncompetitive, weekend cyclist, in reasonable shape, you can figure an average speed along the canal towpaths between 10 and 14 miles per hour. If your objective is simply to finish, you can do any of the three canal routes covered here in less than four days.

But speed isn't the objective of this book nor, hopefully, of the average reader. When something along the way interests you, stop and look. Take detours to visit promising villages or points of interest off the route. Follow a hiking trail, a *randonnée*, off into the countryside. Talk to people. Savor the picturesque cultural differences. Drink in the history and the scenery. Take your time.

Another suggestion: At mid-point of any route, declare a vacation from your vacation, at least one day off for rest, relaxation, and contemplation.

Mileage of the canals covered here is as follows: Brittany, from Pontivy to Nantes, 128; Midi, from Agen to Narbonne, 258; Burgundy, from Dijon to Migennes, 133. Figuring a daily run of 30 miles and a day off in the middle, even the Midi can be comfortably explored in nine days. Three weeks would be a conservative figure for completion of all three routes by even a novice cyclist.

Transport Plans

Working up your transportation plans well in advance can save you money. A good travel agent can save you money by helping you adjust your itinerary to take advantage of the complex fare schedules.

The problem with the system is that travel agents whose compensation is based on maximizing travel costs don't have much incentive for finding bargains.

North American airlines serving France include: American, Canadian Airlines International, Delta, Northwest, TWA, United, and U.S. Airways. Air France also has daily service and Delta flies to Nice as well as Paris. All of these airlines use Charles De-Gaulle Airport (Roissy) with the exception of American, Continental, Delta, and U.S. Airways which use the smaller Orly Airport. Average travel times: from the U.S. East Coast, 8 hours; from Chicago, 9 1/2 hours; from the West Coast, 15 hours. (The Concorde makes the New York-Paris run in just under 4 hours.)

Many seasoned travelers try to fly on weekends when most business travelers stay at home. If you want to try to sleep, you should select a window seat. If you need to circulate, an aisle seat is best. If leg room is a special problem, try for a seat just behind the fuselage door, where once aloft you'll have lots of stretching room. However, your tray service will be a bit awkward and the movie screen may not be visible.

Sometimes price-conscious travelers can find bargains by dealing with consolidators. Consolidators buy blocks of seats from the airlines and resell them at less than list. The Sunday travel section of metropolitan newspapers carry many small ads giving their current discount offerings. Your best bet is to canvass all of them until you find the lowest price for the dates you want to travel. Often the saving will exceed the value of the frequent flyer miles you give up. And not to worry about being canceled at the last minute. Your ticket will be issued by a recognized scheduled airline and will be identical to the one carried by your seatmates who may have spent 40 percent more for the same ride.

Traveling with Children

Don't leave out the kids in your vacation plans. Canal biking is for the whole family, and the kids will love it. On international flights, children under 2 ride free; 2 through 11 usually half price. If an infant accompanies you, check your airline to see if a bulkhead seat and a bassinet can be provided. For more information: Family Travel Times, 40 Fifth Avenue, New York, NY 10011 (Tel. 212-477-5524, fax 212-477-5173).

Air Courier Discounts

If your lifestyle is loose, you keep a packed bag next to your bed, and you have the flexibility to travel on somebody else's schedule, consider being an air courier. These are folks who accompany high-value, time-sensitive shipments in exchange for airfare discounts, sometimes substantial. Often couriers don't even see what it is they are responsible for but their services are important to shippers and courier firms who otherwise could not guarantee speed and reliability of their overseas shipments.

Your dealings will be with courier companies who will sell you your ticket at a discounted rate in exchange for your promise to see that the shipment, sometimes as many as 20 packages, clears customs at the other end and is delivered into the hands of an agent who meets you on the other side of the customs counter. Your return flight, scheduled in advance, also carries the same contractual obligation.

Often you are personally allowed only one or two carry-on bags. The closer to the time of your departure that you make your deal, the larger is your discount. Seldom is a deal set up more than three months in advance. For a list of firms who employ casual couriers, see Appendix D.

Advance Train Travel Arrangements

If your itinerary includes, in addition to your canalside wanderings, extensive European travels, you should consider special rail passes that can be obtained only before you leave the United States. A wide range of options are available. Your travel agent has more information, or write: Rail Europe, 226-230 Westchester Ave., White Plains, NY 10604.

Youth Travel

An International Youth Hostel Membership Card will get you inexpensive, bare-bones accommodation in hostels. However, in France they are found only in major cities. You don't have to be a youth to take advantage. Accommodations are sex-separated dormitories and are available only for night-time use and for a limited stay. Cost per night: $10-$20. Cards cost $25 for adults, $10 for under 18, and $15 for 55 and over. They also provide some transportation discounts. For more information: Hostelling International–American Youth Hostels, 733 15th St. NW, Suite 840, Washington, DC 20005 (Tel. 202-783-6161, fax 202-783-6171) or, in Canada, Hostelling International–Canada, 400-205 Catherine Street, Ottawa, Ontario K2P 1C3 (Tel. 613-237-7884, fax 613-237-7868).

If you are a college student, an International Student Identity Card will provide special rates on transportation, sports events, museums, etc. You need a student I.D. plus $15. Send to Council on International Educational Exchange, 16th Floor, 205 E. 42nd St., New York, NY 10017.

The French rail system has another deal that might fit your needs called Rail 'n' Drive. It provides, at a package discount, three days in one month of unlimited train travel plus three days of Avis car rental.

Car Rental

Gasoline prices in France are about four times the price in the United States. Renting a car is also expensive in France, made even more so by the 18.6 percent tax levied on virtually everything you buy or rent. U.S. rental companies are represented in major cities. For best bargains try Budget and Europcar.

Passports

To enter any foreign country—and more important—to get back into your own, you must have a valid passport. If you don't have one, apply at least five weeks ahead of your planned departure date. If you do have one, be sure to check its expiration date.

Applications

Form DSP-11 for new U.S. passports can be obtained from county courthouses and some post offices. You will need proof of citizenship (either a birth certificate or naturalization papers), proof of identity (driver's license with photo will do) plus two recent 2"x2" head-and-shoulder photos. Your 10-year passport will cost $65 ($40 if you are under 18—for a five-year period). Payment by check, money order, or cash (no change given).

For renewal of existing passport, fill in Form DSP-82 and provide two recent photos plus $55. For more information: Passport Services, U.S. Dept. of State, 1425 K St., Washington, DC 20522.

Canadians can secure their passports through any of 23 regional passport agencies, post offices, or travel agencies. Children traveling with parents can be included on a parent's passport if under 16. Canadian passports are good for five years. For more information: Call 514-283-2152.

It's a good idea to photocopy the I.D. page of your passport and keep it separate from your passport when traveling. Send one also to a relative or friend at home. It may expedite a replacement passport if yours goes missing.

France requires no visa for stays under 90 days.

Money

Plan ahead in order to have access to money during your travels. It is no longer the problem it used to be. U.S. credit cards, particularly Visa *(Carte Bleu)*, are recognized nearly everywhere in France and the easiest way to re-supply cash to your wallet is through cash advance by using your Visa card. ATM machines are everywhere and most accept Visa cards. AmEx cards are accepted at all *Crédit Lyonnais* machines.

If you don't trust credit card financing, traditional traveler's checks, especially Citibank, American Express, and Bank of America, are still widely honored. And they are a good idea if you want to lock in the dollar's present value. Most issuers charge a 1 percent commission. American Express offers traveler's checks, which can be used by each of two traveling companions. Buy them in French francs, not dollars.

It's a good idea to carry some currency with you, U.S. or Canadian, and French, just in case. You can get francs before your departure through your bank or through currency exchange counters at airports. Don't expect the best rate.

Health

If you require special prescription drugs, be sure that you carry with you what you'll require. It's also a good idea to have your doctor note down the generic name of the drugs so that you can replace them if lost or stolen.

Insurance

Consider coverage for health and accident, loss of luggage, flight and trip cancellation. Determine if your existing health insurance policy will cover you in France. Flight insurance (death and dismemberment) is automatically provided when you pay for tickets with some credit cards. Check your homeowner's policy, as it may cover you for lost luggage.

Supplemental health insurance, in case your current policy doesn't cover you abroad, is offered by these companies: Access America (Blue Cross), Box 11188, Richmond, VA 23230; Carefree Travel Insurance, Box 310, 120 Mineola Blvd., Mineola, NY (Tel. 800-323-3149, fax 516-294-1096); International SOS Assistance, Inc., Box 11568, Philadelphia, PA 19116 (Tel. 800-523-8930, fax 215-244-2227, e-mail sosphila@ix.netcom.com); Travel Guard International, 1145 Clark St., Stevens Point, WI 54481 (Tel. 715-345-0505, fax 715-345-0525); Wallach & Co, Box 480, Middleburg, VA 22117-0480 (Tel. 800-237-6615, fax 540-687-3172); Teletrip Co., Inc., P.O. Box 31685, Omaha, NE 68131 (Tel. 800-228-9792).

Canadians are advised not to depend on their Provincial Health Plan to cover sickness or injury abroad. They should purchase supplemental insurance and carry proof with them.

Concerned about your health and how to find an English-speaking doctor in France? Lists of qualified doctors who speak English are available by writing International Association for Medical Assistance to Travelers, 417 Center St., Lewiston, NY 14092 (Tel. 716-754-4883, e-mail iamat@sentex.net) or in Canada at 40 Regal Rd., Guelph, Ont., N1K 1B5 (Tel. 519-836-0102, fax 519-836-3412).

What You Can Bring into France

French customs regulations are not as strict as those of the United States, but there are a few restrictions: a maximum of 400 cigarettes, 100 cigars, two liters of wine, one liter of alcohol.

Chapter 2

What to Take

There's an axiom among long-distance cyclers: Everything that rides with you has to pay its way. If it doesn't, it should stay at home or be jettisoned en route.

Clothing needs along your bike route will be minimal. Choose fast-drying fabrics like synthetics or synthetic-cotton blends. Avoid wool.

Most important: a light nylon windbreaker with inside and outside closeable pockets. Helmets are not required in France; some cyclists don't bother with them even on highways. A light hat with a visor takes a lot less room. Foul-weather suits? A tossup. They take a lot of space and the few that are really effective are very expensive.

There's no need to carry different soaps for different chores. Woolite works well as a shampoo, for personal bathing, clothes washing, and dishwashing. It's available everywhere.

A set of street clothes is included because the French have a tendency to dress more formally than Americans. Shorts and bike touring clothes might not be suitable for a movie theater, cathedral tour, or monastery visit.

Another important item: money belt or belly pouch to secure passport, credit cards, cash, and traveler's checks. Be sure that your passport, credit card, and traveler's check numbers are logged elsewhere, just in case.

Distance bikers tend to become obsessive about their packs and panniers, assigning to each a specific list of items and almost always in a specific order, with items most often used stashed near the top. Many roll individual items of clothing tightly and stuff them into Ziploc bags to keep them dry. Often a handlebar pannier is designated for valuable and active items like cameras, maps, guide books, and other items likely to be needed en route. Panniers ought to carry your name and address—why not in day-glo lettering?

Speaking strictly about your needs for canal cycling as separate from an evening gown for a Paris ball or golf clubs for a Scottish detour, here is a suggested checklist:

Fat-tired bicycle,
   with horn or bell
Passport
Credit card(s) and/or
   traveler's checks plus
   francs and dollars
Insurance credentials
Air tickets
Two changes of bike
   riding clothes
One set of street clothes
Sweater
Light rain suit (optional)
Shoes
Light jacket with zip or
   buttoned pockets
Gloves
Hat or helmet
Body pouch for cash,
   valuables
Address book
Glasses
Sunglasses
Pocket French-English
   dictionary

Toilet paper
Emergency rations: dried
   fruit, trail mix, candy bars
Playing cards
Multipurpose jack knife
Compass
Length of clothesline, pins
First-aid kit
Bungee cord
Toilet kit, including soap
   box, toothbrush, toothpaste,
   floss, razor, blades, comb
Towel
Self-closing plastic bags for
   separating and
   waterproofing clothing
Water bottle(s)
Journal/log book
Net shopping bag
Watch or travel alarm clock
Pen
Flashlight (small)
This book

Bike checklist:
Panniers
Spare tube
Tire pump
All-purpose bike tool
Spoke wrench
Spare spokes

Tube repair kit
Bike lock and cable
Chain lube
Spare brake pads
Gel seat cushion if
   butt-sensitive

If you plan to camp:
Tent
Ground cloth
Sleeping bag

Propane cook stove
Pot, pan, utensils
Lighter

Some other items to consider:
Video or still camera
Small binoculars
Audio recorder for taking notes

Miniature radio
Pocket calculator

220- to 110-volt converter (with French plug)
if you need to run hair dryer, shaver, or
battery charger

First-aid kit contents:

Sunscreen	Chap Stick
Band Aids or gauze and tape for dressings	Pain reliever
	Athlete's foot remedy
Antibiotic ointment	Space blanket
Anti-diarrheal treatment	Any special medication you need
Rantex, talc, or ointment for butt problems	

Some other items to carry along:

Flexibility	Sense of humor
Like-minded companion	

Togetherness versus Solo

A compatible companion may be the most important item of all. Solo, the canals are fun, but with a compatible companion, the pleasure quotient is synergistic. A partner helps in decision making, provides a sounding board and companionship. If your partner is fluent in French, all the better. And traveling with another means that many of the items on the checklist can be shared, as well as housekeeping duties, too.

Remember, most Americans tend to carry too much with them when they travel. They forget that Europeans have access to everything we have. If you turn up at the start of your canal ride having left something vital at home on the kitchen table, there will be a store around the corner with what you need. Exceptions: maple syrup and chunky peanut butter.

Some other packing tips: If you are cycling in mid-summer you may not need a full rain suit. Leave the pants at home, save space, and ride with damp legs for a while. Avoid cotton underwear as it promotes chafing. Instead wear synthetic or silk. Use miniature sizes of toilet items to conserve space.

Start Getting in Shape

If you are equipping yourself with new or familiar equipment before leaving for France, take time to flight test it under a full pack. Learn how to handle a loaded bike, how much longer it takes to stop one, particularly in the rain. Exercise it and yourself on a short tour so you know what to expect. Get your legs, butt, and the rest of your body in shape by jogging, racquetball, swimming, or using a stationary bike.

Chapter 3

Your Mount: To Accompany or Acquire?

A s *Business Week* said in a recent article about a new type of folding bike, "Traveling on a bicycle is great fun. Traveling with a bicycle is a great big headache." Because of this truism, deciding whether to take a bike or acquire one abroad is a basic one. Here are some options on how you can arrive at your starting point, bike in hand. You have three main possibilities:

(1) Bring one from home.
(2) Rent one in France, either in Paris or at your start-off point.
(3) Buy one in France, either in Paris or at your start-off point.
Let's deal with each in turn.

Bringing One From Home

The principal problem has to do with a bicycle's innate awkwardness in being packed into a suitcase. The advantage is that it's a friend: comfortable, familiar, and predictable.

Most airlines may not be overjoyed, but they will accept a bicycle and limited liability. But in doing so you use up one of your two allowed checked pieces of baggage. You can decide to provide your own carrying box or bag (a friendly bike shop may help) or you can usually count on your airline having one. If you are going to commit the problem to the airline and you arrive with a bare bike, leave plenty of time for them to package it. It would be well to have the tools with you to loosen the handle bars and remove the pedals. Ticket agents are not handy with tools.

Most airlines will provide a box, and most will charge you for it, but usually only $10 or $15. Always check with them in advance to be sure they have them in stock.

If you pack your bike, its container has to be within 62 inches in length, width, and girth combined. The airline will count your bicycle as one of your two allowed 70-pound pieces of checked baggage even though it may gross only half of that; thus, if you are doing your own packing, you might want to use any extra space to accommodate other belongings. You also are allowed one or two pieces of carry-on, up to a maximum of 40 pounds. Be careful of being over the weight limit; it can be expensive.

Another solution to this and the subsequent problem of getting your cycle into taxis, buses, and trains is a hard-sided bike case or canvas bike bag with sturdy carrying handles that, once the front wheel and pedals are removed and handle bar swung, takes up only the space of a suitcase. See Chapter 4 and Appendix 6 for more details.

At Paris Airports

You'll save time and hassle if you arrange to transfer on from Paris to the airport closest to your cycling departure point. However, if a Paris stopover is a must you have several choices to get yourself and your bike into the city.
(1) Taxi. Try to find a station wagon taxi that can take the packed bike on its roof or in the back.
(2) Airport buses have space in their baggage compartments but you should be at the front of the line to make stowage easier. Unpack it in the city center upon arrival and ride to your hotel.
(3) Unpack your bike and ride it to the suburban rail line on the airport grounds. During off-peak hours you can stow it in the front of the car you're riding in.
(4) Ride your bike into the city, trying to avoid busy superhighways.

The thought of riding Paris streets may challenge your courage at first, but it is really the most efficient means of getting around. Almost always you'll get where you're going faster than if you were driving. Courage will also come from watching Parisian housewives making their way through traffic on prewar single speeds, their panniers loaded with cabbages, sausages, and wine from the market. If you are still apprehensive, choose a Sunday morning for your first foray. You'll have Paris all to yourself.

Getting out of Paris is not as daunting a task as you might think. The French national railway system (SNCF), which reaches to every corner of the country with some of the best service in the world, claims to have a soft spot in its heart for cyclists.

Usually bicycles are allowed with you free on local trains. They aren't permitted on the superfast TGV or other express trains. Check your timetables; the trains with a sketch of a bicycle are those you want. Most suburban Paris trains take bicycles except during peak times (6:30-9:30 A.M. and 4:30-7:00 P.M.) No problem Saturdays, Sundays and bank holidays.

It's your responsibility to load the bike and to be sure it doesn't block the aisle. Often there is space in the vestibule, but

25

it's best to have some bungee cord to keep it in place. Sometimes bicycles will be accepted in the baggage car, but here again, it is your responsibility to load and unload.

You can also ship your bicycle as ordinary baggage. It may arrive two or three days after you do and the charge will be based on mileage.

Renting a Bike in France

Most moderate-sized cities in France have sophisticated bicycle specialty dealers and most of them offer rental bikes. In remote areas your choice will usually be more limited than in Paris or other metropolitan areas. Expect to pay $175–$225 for a two-week rental plus a deposit of about $300. (See Appendix 4 for a list of rental firms in Paris and the three regions covered or write the local tourist office for additional names.)

The French railroads are also in the bicycle rental business with rental bikes in about 50 stations around the country. Equipment condition and quality vary.

A problem with rental bikes is that you have to return them to your starting point unless you are able to make special arrangements. Try to arrange to ship the bike back as train baggage with the understanding that your deposit will be mailed to you upon receipt. Otherwise, you can double back or accompany the bike back by train.

Buying a Bike in France

This has the advantage that you don't have to encumber yourself en route, and that you can choose what suits you best. If you make a ship-back, buy-back deal with the merchant in advance, you may not need to be encumbered on the return.

Another advantage over bringing your own bike with you: the bike you buy will be a French bike, well known to mechanics in even the smallest village. Spare parts won't be a problem.

Don't worry about bicycle quality or varieties available or the state of French bike technology. Cycling is a French national way of life as well as a national sport. The *Tour de France* is France's Rose Bowl, World Series, and PGA golf tourney rolled into one.

Chapter 4

About Bicycles

O nly one rule is absolute to negotiate the changeable terrain encountered along the canals: Leave your skinny-tired racing bike at home. Beyond that, any reasonably sturdy hybrid or mountain bike will get you where you want to go. Obviously, a state-of-the-art titanium and balsa mountain bike that has 38 speeds, radar, power brakes and whistles, and weighs under 10 pounds might make the work easier. But it's up to you to determine its cost effectiveness.

Because of the unique absence of hills, state-of-the-art multispeed transmissions are not important to the canalside cyclist. You may set the speed at a comfortable rate and leave it there untouched for the rest of the day, unless a companion challenges you to a race or you leave the canal path for supplies or exploration.

Bike Packs

If you plan to stay exclusively in hotels or guest houses and thus have no need of cumbersome tents or sleeping bags, you can probably get by with panniers straddling the back wheel plus a handlebar bag and a belly pack for your valuables. If you plan to camp, figure front wheel panniers as well.

Seats

This may be one of your most important decisions. It should not be summarily dismissed without investigation and trial. The seat will be your body's most intimate companion for many hours. It does not have to be a torture rack, particularly if you are prepared. Most of the discomfort felt in this region comes from the tailbones not being accustomed to heavy use in this way. Without any help, they will adapt naturally in two or three weeks. The problem is that if your ride of a lifetime lasts only two or three weeks, there can be painful experiences.

One way around it, of course, is to acclimate yourself in practice sessions before you start. Another is to buy a seat that has gel padding built in. A separate gel cover is available for existing seats, as are bike pants with built-in pads.

The problem may be more important for women, as their physiology requires a wider, shorter seat than is comfortable for a man. It all boils down to trying out seats in advance until you find one that works best for you.

Bike Carrying Cases and Bags

As discussed in Part V, Chapter 3, most airlines provide packing boxes for bikes at a nominal charge. They are usually a one-time solution, and if you are fussy, not usually entirely damage-proof. There are two other more permanent solutions to the ever-present problem of taking your bike with you on public or private transportation: soft-sided bags and rigid cases.

Neither is cheap, and both have drawbacks and require extensive disassembly and re-assembly.

The major problem with soft-sided bags is that they don't provide much protection against muscular baggage handlers. Their advantage is that the bag can be folded and easily carried along for re-use at the end of the bike ride. They are cheaper than hard-sided cases. If you choose a soft case, it's a good idea to insert a spacer between the forks to add rigidity when the wheels are removed.

Rigid cases are usually made of reinforced plastic and come with handles, hasps for locking, and have fitted interiors. They are usually favored by professionals and racers who are interested in maximum protection. The big problem is what to do with the empty case when you get to the start of your cycling and ride off into the sunset. This problem has recently been addressed by at least two manufacturers, who now offer a shipping case that converts into a baggage trailer. Most hard cases come with wheels for trundling down airport corridors. See Appendix 6 for a list of manufacturers of cases and bags.

Whichever type you buy, it's a good idea to have a supply of zip ties or heavy tape to aid in packing. Be sure your case or bag is well marked with your name and address. It's also a good idea to keep air in the tires when you pack them, but they should not be fully inflated or you will have a blowout at altitude.

Rules of the Road

While most of your ride will be traffic-free, here are some road rules for those times when you have to conduct yourself as a responsible highway user:

- Stay on the extreme right edge of the road, except when you are in a right turn lane and want to go left or straight ahead.
- Always signal in advance for right or left turns. If you plan to slow or stop, signal with your left arm at less than 90 degrees.
- Watch out for traffic from the right. In France, traffic on the right has the right of way unless you are on a "yellow diamond" major highway.
- When making a left turn, wait until all approaching traffic has cleared the intersection.
- Ride single file in populated areas.
- Give pedestrians right of way, especially in crosswalks.
- Obey all signs, including one-way streets, and don't ride in bus lanes, sidewalks, or on superhighways.
- Don't run stop lights or stop signs.
- In wet conditions, allow much more time to stop, especially when your bike is heavily loaded.
- Reduce tire pressure on rough surfaces to increase comfort. Do not reduce it below the lowest number printed on the side of the tire, or you will have puncture problems.

Sizing a Bike

Having a bike that fits is important. There are several methods of fitting, and the fussier you are, the more complex the formula. The simplest method is to straddle the horizontal bar in front of the seat. Lift the bike as high as it will go. If there are 4 to 6 inches of clearance between the bike tires and the ground, it is about right—for a mountain bike. For a road bike, the clearance should be 1 to 2 inches.

Another method is to place your feet 10 inches apart. Measure the distance from your crotch to the floor and multiply that by .68. This should be your proper bike size in inches. To convert to metric equivalent, see the metric conversion tables in Appendix 2.

More complex formulae that involve your weight, age, muscle tone, and phase of the moon exist for those who enjoy that sort of thing.

Bike Repairs Along the Way

Your most likely problem will be a flat tire. Always carry a patching kit or replacement tube or both, tools for getting the tube off, and a pump. Finding tubes and tires to U.S. specifications in small villages may not be easy.

Potholes or errant tree roots can put a wheel out of round. If on your own without a mechanic handy, you should have a spoke wrench and know the basics for effecting on-the-spot repairs. It's a good idea to carry a couple of spare spokes. You should know that for each spoke that's adjusted, the spoke next to it, which goes to the opposite hub flange, has to be turned in the opposite direction. For instance, if you tighten one spoke to pull the rim in a direction to straighten it, you should loosen the spoke next to it by the same amount to maintain even tension.

It's not likely that your brake pads will need replacement, but just in case, new pads don't take up much space and a loaded bike without good brakes can ruin a whole day. Be sure the brake pads are properly aligned on the rims. Adjustments to the derailleur cables may be necessary. Be sure your kit contains the necessary tools.

Glossary of Bike Terms

Here are some French words and terms that might be useful in a cycle shop:

J'ai besoin de	jay beh zwan deh	I need—
le guidon	leh gwee dohn	handlebars
le frein	leh freh	brake
le rayon	leh ray ohn	spoke
cassé	cah say	broken
les pignons	lay pee nyon	sprockets
la selle	la sell	seat
la chambre d'aire	la chahm breh dare	tube
le pneu	leh new	tire
le nécessaire de réparation	leh neh sehs air deh rep ar ah sion	tire kit repair(ing)
le vélo	leh vay low	bicycle
VTT	vay tay tay	mountain bike
le cable	leh cah ble	cable
le chain	leh shehn	chain
le guarde bou	leh gard boo	fender
l'écrou	lay crew	nut
la sacoche	la sah kawsh	pannier
la pédale	la pay doll	pedal
la pompe	la pohmp	pump
le tournevis	leh tour neh veez	screwdriver
la vis	la veez	screw
le clé	leh klay	wrench
le clé hex	leh klay hex	hex wrench
la roue	la roo	wheel

Chapter 5

Accommodations—
A Pillow for Your Head

The French countryside you will be passing through offers adequate, if not always sumptuous, overnight accommodation. Your choices along the canals will range from simple hotels to even more simple guest houses to campgrounds plus an occasional luxurious *château*. But whichever you choose, as a cycler you will almost always be given a hearty welcome, a clean bed, usually a good meal, and a safe place for your bike.

Hotels

Small, family-owned hotels still survive in France, and they are surprisingly numerous, even in the remote backcountry. They are comfortable, inexpensive, and almost always clean. Most offer excellent meals and bar facilities. Most have less than 20 rooms. Rooms with baths or showers and toilets are in the minority, but those offering one of the above can usually be found. Often the missing facility is just down the hall.

You will not find it difficult, even today, to find a country hotel room for 180 francs (about $36) per night. That price holds whether there are one, two, or three occupants, and it may include continental breakfast. A four-star *château* may cost 600-700 francs (about $120-140) per night. Most hotels today accept major credit cards and traveler's checks.

Usually language won't be a problem. Hotel managers deal with other languages more intimately than anybody else in a country village. They may not be able to discuss politics with you, but they almost always understand what you need.

In towns, direction signs will point to the major hotels. Don't reject a hotel because it is in a poorer section or near the railroad station. Often that's where the best values are. A *Hôtel de Commerce* is where the salesmen stay. If a sign proclaims it is a *Logis de France*, it is a part of a 5,000-member syndicate of family-owned hostelries that are usually charming, upscale, and cater to the tourist. For information and a list of member hotels: Logis de France, 25 Rue de Jean Mermoz, 75008 Paris.

Relais et Châteaux is another syndication, an even more up-market offering of renovated manor houses and *châteaux*.

French hotels are graded by stars; theoretically, the more displayed, the higher the standards. Along the canal paths, hotels will usually be two-star, one-star, and unrated. Often the differences will be difficult to discern, even after you've received the bill, at least until you get to the three-star category.

Some special tips about French country hotels: Bear in mind that every Frenchman and his family gets out of Paris and the other major cities for a month-long summer vacation. Accommodations can be scarce, particularly during the peak between July 15 and August 15. Always try to plan your day's itinerary and call ahead for reservations at least before you start your day's run. Even on either side of the peak period, it's a good idea. The hotel will usually take your word for it and will hold your room at least until 6 P.M. If there is reluctance, give your credit card number.

If you forget, however, and you need help, you can always appeal to the local tourist office. One of their main jobs is to see that tourists are accommodated. There is no charge except for toll calls, when necessary, but a dish for tips is usually on the counter. Every office has at least one person who speaks English. Be aware, though, that most tourist offices close by 5 P.M.

Out in the country, folks have a habit of retiring early—hotelkeepers, too. If you plan to be out, ask when they lock the front door. They'll provide a key if you request it, or a combination number for an electronic lock. Don't forget—a locked and dark hotel at midnight can be an unpleasant prospect.

The French are more frugal than Americans about lights. At night upstairs hallways and stairways are as dark as the inside of a coal mine. The reason: the lights are on a timer. Look for the light switch, usually luminescent, to light your way, but hurry; it will go out soon.

Continental plumbing is generally a generation behind American. Showers are usually unsatisfactory, if you are of normal height, unless you enjoy flooded bathroom floors. Are French plumbers midgets? The showerheads seem to be only belly-button height on most Americans. French plumbing valves have an irritating habit of closing down on their own, causing alternate freezing and scalding. Another caution: The strange device next to the toilet isn't. It is a bidet (bee day), a device for bathing nether regions. (Useful, too, for washing socks and underwear.)

For the devotee of reading in bed there are two common problems: inadequate reading light and a strange pillow configuration that won't get your head high enough for comfort. Kind words to the management may produce a reading lamp and a second pillow—in French, *lumière* (loom ee yair) and *oreiller* (or ee yay) respectively.

In most French hotels, it doesn't matter if the room has one or two or more occupants, as the price is by the room. The official price is always posted on the room door. Sometimes a dicker will work, and you can negotiate a discount, particularly if business is slow. Suggestion: total the room price, breakfast and dinner price, and offer 20 percent less. It may be accepted, or you may get a counter offer.

During negotiation, there is no rule that says you can't ask to inspect the room. Some innkeepers may offer the room *demi-pension* only. That means that having your evening meal in house is obligatory. Beware.

In French villages and small towns, the wake-up sounds you hear from your hotel room window are a part of the special color of the country: the greetings of housewives and shopkeepers, the sound of brooms sweeping the sidewalks and gutters, the squeaking and clatter of shutters being opened, the bang of trash cans being loaded into refuse trucks, the buzzing of motorbikes carrying kids to school. Speaking of sounds, it's a good idea to have a room far removed from the elevator. It often clangs and clatters.

Motels are on the increase in France, but they lack the ambiance, the menu, and the personal touch of the small country hotel. Least expensive of these is the automated Formula 1 chain, in which employees are as scarce as the ambiance. The rock-bottom price includes up to three per room.

Guest Houses

The French call them *chambres d'hôte* (shahm breh doat). They are basically private homes set up to take a limited number of guests, often open only during the high season. You will usually be offered breakfast, but not necessarily any other meal. Usually, the price will be less than a room in a hotel.

Hostels

These were originally meant for collegiates traveling on the cheap. Unfortunately in France, they are hard to find outside of the larger cities. If you do find one and have the requisite Hostel Association membership card, age is no problem, although noise and confusion may be. Many have an early curfew and are not open at all during the day. Maximum stay is three days. A sleeping bag is required. In warm weather a pouch made of two single bedsheets sewn together is best.

Camping

The French are inveterate campers, and you will find municipal, regional, and private campgrounds almost everywhere. Watch out, though; many are open only May through September. A few go year-round.

French campsites are universally well managed. Like hotels, they have been rated upon their location and facilities; the more stars the better the scenery and the more amenities offered.

Unlike many private campgrounds in the United States that cater only to RVs, French campgrounds accommodate tenters as well. They offer a varied list of facilities. Nearly always you'll get a plot for your tent, clean toilets, showers, and a place to wash clothes at a surprisingly inexpensive price. Availability of electricity, swimming, tennis, restaurant, provisions, maybe.

An average charge per tent for a night will be a couple of dollars plus perhaps another dollar for hot water. Even when the sign *complet* (kahm pleh) indicates no more room, space for a tent can almost always be found.

For a list of sites and more specific information: Fédération Française de Camping et Caravaning, 78 Rue de Rivoli, 75004 Paris.

Some farmers have entered the camping business, offering an unofficial back meadow for campers. The amenities will be few, but the ambiance interesting. Look for signs: *Camping à la Ferme.*

On the Water

Your route will take you past a number of rental boat headquarters. If other lodgings are unavailable, check with the boat rental company for accommodation on a boat for the night.

Holiday barges, too, are a part of the canal side scenery. They are in the business of taking guests for longer than overnight, but still, if there is space available, they might be able to solve a problem. Accommodations, food, and their charges will be first class. Occasionally, lockkeepers make rooms available for transients.

In the Wild

Cyclists along the canals are not encouraged to camp in the wild, but if you are more than one mile from a highway or public accommodation, no one will blow a whistle. Where possible, always ask permission of the property owner and, of course, leave no trash.

Mountain Shelters

These are called *abris* (ahb ree) and they are just simple shelters for backpackers and climbers in mountainous areas. They have practically no amenities, but are inexpensive, friendly, and almost always have terrific views. In the event you want to take a detour from the canal towpath and need a shelter, check the tourist offices for *abris* along your route.

Rental Cottages

Almost every region of the country is a target for vacationers, and charming, fully equipped, self-catering cottages and farmhouses are available most everywhere. It may suit your plans to take a week or more to stop en route to smell the roses. Tourist offices can help. These rental units are called *gites* (jeet) or if more bare bones, *gites d'étape* (jeet day tahp).

A Hotel Glossary

Here are some French terms and words that you may encounter when dealing with accommodations:

Auberge	oh bearj	Inn, usually in the country
Gite or Gite d'étape	jeet, jeet day tahp	Vacation rental cottage, usually by the week or longer
Chambre d'hôte	shahm breh doat	Guest house
Relais	reh lay	Roadside inn, often favored by truckers
Complet	kahm pleh	Sold out, no room at the inn
Etage	ay tahj	Floor. If your room is on the *deuxième étage*, you are on what the French call the second floor. Actually, you are on the third floor as the French numbers start with the floor above the ground floor.
Douche	doush	Shower, usually without proper shower curtain

Bain, salle de bain	beh, sahl deh beh	Bath, bathroom. May or may not have a WC or toilet
Chambre	shahm breh	Room
Chambre pour deux personnes	shahm breh poor deh pair son	Double room
Petit déjeuner	pet ee day jeh nay	Breakfast
Petit déjeuner inclus	pet ee day jeh nay en clou	Breakfast included in room price
Garage pour vélo	gay raj poor vay low	Place to put the bicycle
Facture	fahk tyur	Hotel bill
Moins chère	moh aah shair	Something cheaper, as in "Do you have a cheaper room?"
Escalier	es kahl yay	Stairway
Le clé	leh klay	Key

Turrets, buttresses, and gargoyles reaching back through the ages are the marks of French church architecture.

Chapter 6

Not by Bread Alone— Food and Wine

If what you eat and drink holds special importance for you, you are coming to the right place. In France, somebody counted 450 different kinds of cheeses alone. France also boasts an astronomical number of wine labels, as well as the largest supply of the world's most pricey food item, the truffle.

The French have taken eating to an art form, think nothing of devoting three or four hours to a Sunday meal. And nowhere is this worship of the taste buds more evident than in the countryside.

Not only is French cuisine distinctive, often a model for the rest of the civilized world, but within France, you will find a staggering array of regional specialties. Along the Canal du Midi, in the area of Castelnaudary, a stew called *cassoulet* is ubiquitous. Across the mountains of the Massif Central in Dijon, stew is also a specialty, but there it is called *boeuf bourguignon*. Both have many common ingredients, but there the similarity stops. Nuances are everything in what the French put past their taste buds.

But the French are not only gourmets with the ability to sort out all of these nuances, they are also gourmands, approaching a meal with undisguised zeal and huge appetites. Don't get in their way.

Dinner in France begins about 8 P.M. Few hotel dining rooms or restaurants will open before 7:00.

A meal in a good restaurant or in a friend's house is a bit more complex than you may be accustomed to. The French frown upon cocktails before a meal, holding that strong liquor deadens the taste. Instead, you will be offered an *apéritif*, a much less alcoholic drink, with a few crackers or peanuts.

The apéritif may be *kir* or *kir royale*. Principal ingredient is a liqueur made from currants and mixed with either a white still wine or champagne, thus, royale. You might be offered *pastis*, an anise-flavored drink favored in the south of the country; *suze*, made from gentian, a bittersweet mountain herb; or *martini*, not the gin-type, but a white vermouth. In addition, there are scores of strictly local concoctions.

After the social *apéritif* it's time for the serious business. First, there is the *entrée*, which in French means the beginning. It usually features raw vegetables, *crudités*, or perhaps oysters or other seafood. The main course features some type of meat in a hearty sauce, plus potatoes and vegetables. Then there may be a fish course, likewise in a savory sauce. The salad course is next, followed by a cheese plate with a dizzying variety of hard and soft cheeses. A large basket of bread, crusty outside, soft inside, comes with the cheese. Dessert, coffee, and a *digestif* follows. *Digestif* is what we would call an after-dinner drink, usually cognac or a liqueur.

Wine is served throughout the meal; the varieties, quality, and age depend on the bank balance of your host, or if on your own in a restaurant, your own. Some restaurants, usually the bargain ones, advertise *boisson compris*. That means you get a carafe of house wine without extra charge.

When you order water, *l'eau* (it seldom is served unless requested), you will normally get bottled water. If you don't want it bubbly, *gazeuse*, ask specifically for *l'eau plate*. There is a charge for bottled water, none for tap water, a *carafe d'eau*.

Most of the small country inns along canal routes will offer you an evening meal. Don't expect a complex menu. But even in the outback, sauces accompany the main course. The sauce is what gives the chef his special credentials.

You should be warned that in France, meat, particularly beef, is served several shades to the left of very rare. To talk the chef into what we call "cooked" is a challenge. It may not help, but here are some adjectives in case you can find a chef who will listen:

Americans call it:	*French call it:*	
Medium	Bien cuit	byen cwee
Rare	a point	ah pwahnt
Barely warm	Saignant*	say nyant

*What you usually get if you remain mute.
Note: There is no expression in French for well done.

Vegetables will usually come fresh from the garden behind the kitchen door or were brought on a bicycle pedaled by madame from the market this morning.

Desserts in most country hotels usually consist of several flavors of ice cream. The French hotel industry leaves fancy pastries and desserts to their brothers in the *cafés* or *brasseries* (bars that offer short-order meals). If the inn hasn't satisfied your sweet tooth, just walk across the street.

Many Americans have a problem with the thick, strong French espresso-type coffee. To Americanize it, call for *café au lait*, which will come in a familiar-size cup with steamed milk.

Regardless of what the movie script writers say, French waiters should never be called *garçon*. Try *Monsieur*, or if female, *Madame*.

The French give small emphasis to breakfast, *petit déjeuner*. What you receive just off the lobby of most country hotels will be the same as it was the day before 30 miles back. It will unerringly consist of juice or fruit, fresh bread and a croissant, butter (not margarine), jam, cheese or honey, and coffee or tea. You won't complain after you have bitten into the still warm goddess of all pastries, the croissant, and the bread, both of which were in the baker's oven only minutes before.

If you are looking for a good restaurant in a strange town, head for the older section of town. It is here that the restaurants, nightclubs, and bars are thickest. Here, too, you'll usually find a good mix of ethnic eateries, almost always Chinese, Vietnamese, Italian, Greek, and North African. If Tex-Mex is your obsession, you may have a problem. Perhaps you should try Spanish.

Out on the canal path it is unlikely that you'll starve. For lunch you don't need to find a restaurant. Any *café-bar* will provide a *sandwich*, pronounced "sahn VEECH." What you get will be half of a small loaf of bread cut the long way and stuffed with cheese, ham, sausage, or tomatoes or all of the above. Try a *croque monsieur*, a super grilled ham and cheese sandwich. A *croque madame* is the same augmented by an egg.

In *café-bars* and *brasseries*, particularly in towns and cities, there is usually a service surcharge for sitting at a table. Sit at the bar for the best bargain. A specialty is *choucroute*, sauerkraut with sausage, or a wide diversity of omelets or salads. In a French bar or restaurant you may pay more for bottled water or a cola drink than you will for wine.

If you encounter an inn or restaurant at your mid-day stop, and need more than a sandwich, the full meal you get will be a bargain. Noon meals are at least as prodigious as evening meals and the price is better.

If economy is important, look for restaurants offering a blue plate special, in French, a *prix fixe* meal. The package price will be prominently displayed outside the restaurant and usually reflects what bargains the chef found in the market that morning.

Ordering *à la carte* is much more expensive. And remember that restaurants are open only at mealtimes and often are closed by 10 P.M.

Do-it-yourself trail meals can be routine, too. Before setting off, stop at the bakery, *boulangerie*, for a loaf of fresh bread; at the specialty store, *charcuterie*, for a ready-made salad, cold cuts, and nibble items; and almost anywhere for a bottle of wine or soft drink. Where can you stop for a picnic? Obviously you wouldn't choose someone's front walk or the cathedral steps, but almost anywhere else and you won't be criticized. Even the smallest village has a public park with picnic tables.

You'll be surprised how a picnic table can materialize right along the path. If one doesn't, just find a convenient tree to lean against.

Watch out for the French custom, particularly in the country, of closing almost everything down at noon, often for two hours or more. This includes supermarkets, bakeries, fruiterers—virtually everything except restaurants and bars. On Sunday morning, most shops dealing in food stay open until noon to catch the church crowd.

Americans tend to think of the barbecue as an American tradition. Maybe so, but we have no claim to its origination. The word barbecue comes from the French *barbe*, beard, and *queue*, tail. Literally, spit-cooking an animal from beard to tail.

A word of caution: The French have a quiet, on-going war against litter and trash. Wherever you stop, leave it at least as clean as when you arrived.

What to do about wine, soft drink, and water bottles? Recycling has arrived in France and most communities have large, round containers near the town center for that purpose. Or carry the bottles with you until you find a trash bin, in French, a *poubelle*. In the United States, there are pick-up campaigns to dispose of highway litter. In France litter doesn't seem to happen in the first place.

Today nearly every city, town, and village in France has its new and brassy supermarket, which physically looks a lot like where you shop at home. They come with names like: *Mammouth, LeClerc, Intermarché,* and *Casino.* The offerings and business customs are different, however.

The French *supermarché* provides its customers with the same kind of shopping carts as its American counterpart, but in France you need to insert a 10-franc coin in a slot on the handle to free it from its chain. When you are finished, take it back, reattach the chain, and the coin will be returned to you. The system keeps the parking lot free of clutter.

In fresh fruit and vegetable departments, put the merchandise you select into a plastic bag, put the bag on the scales and punch a button labeled with the name of its item. *Voila!* Out comes a sticky-backed price label for your bag. But you don't know the French word for artichoke? No problem! Each item is pictured on its button.

The least expensive wine is that which you can buy in a supermarket in unlabeled liter bottles with stars on their necks. Many stores have wine on tap for folks who bring their own bottles.

At the checkout, your credit card is usually as acceptable as cash, but you'll need your passport for verification. French housewives who pay with a check don't even have to make it out. Their blank check is automatically filled in by the cash register. The customer just signs and walks out.

Glossary

Some French terms you may encounter in connection with eating and drinking:

Brasserie	brah sar ee	Restaurant featuring bar plus short-order meals, omelets, steaks and french fries (*frites*), salads, etc.
Café-bar	cah fay bar	Bar plus snacks, sandwiches
Bar	bar	Just that
Grillade au feu de bois	gree ahd oh fou deh bwah	charcoal broiled
Prix fixe	pree feeks	Blue plate or chef's special, may or may not include table wine
Service compris/ non compris	sair vees comp ree	Tip is included in the price—or not. Mostly it is, except in bars
Viande	vee yahnd	Meat
Steak	stek	Steak
Steak haché	stek hahsh ay	Hamburger
Poisson	pwah son	Fish
Légumes	lay goum	Vegetables
Pain, Petit pain	pehn, pet tee pehn	Bread, rolls
Beurre	burr	Butter
Sel et poivre	sell ay pwahv	Salt and pepper

Fromage	fro mahj	Cheese
Potage, soupe	poh tahj, soup	Soup
L'eau, l'eau plat	low, low plaht	Water, bottled water without carbonation
Café	cah fay	Espresso
Café au lait	cah fay oh lay	Coffee with steamed milk. If you want American coffee, ask for Nescafé.
Bière	bee air	Beer
Bière pression	bee air presh yon	Draft beer
Martini	mar teen ee	Vermouth, a fortified wine. If you want a martini cocktail, ask for *gin martini*. Not usually satisfactory to the connoisseur.
Cognac ar monyak	coh nyak,	French types of Ar magnac brandy
Kir, kir royale	keer, keer roy all	Before dinner drinks, *apéritifs*. *Kir* is a currant liqueur mixed with white wine; *royale*, with champagne.
Vin, vin blanc, vin rouge,	van, blahnk, rooj,	Wine, white wine, red wine
Vin maison, vin ordinaire	may zon, ordin air	house wine, cheap wine.
Ferme auberge	fairm oh bearj	Farm restaurant specializing in fresh, homegrown items. Usually limited menu.
Bon appétit	bohn ah pet eat	Have a good meal.
L'addition	la dis yon	The bill (restaurant)
Combien?	com byen	How much?
s'il vous plaît	on core see vou play	Encore, Another of the same, please

Chapter 7

Transport— How to Get Around

G etting around in France is probably easier than in any other country in the world, thanks to its super efficient rail system. In France, if your watch shows that your train is late, it's probably your watch that's wrong.

From the Airport into Paris

You can get into Paris from either Charles DeGaulle (Roissy) or Orly Airport by taxi, bus, or train. Allow about 45 minutes to an hour, no matter which mode you choose. At both airports, free shuttle buses take you from your arrival building to the train station on the airport perimeter. At DeGaulle go to Door 30 and watch for buses marked "Roissy Rail." You buy your rail ticket at the rail station.

At Orly look for the gate marked, "Sortie aux Autocars et Navettes." Nearby is a booth where you must buy your rail ticket. Then look for the bus marked, "Orly Rail." The shuttle buses in both airports are fast and efficient, leave about every 15 minutes. From DeGaulle your train will arrive at Paris' Gare du Nord. From Orly you arrive at Gare d'Austerlitz.

In addition, direct bus service from both airports into the center of the city is operated by Air France.

Rail Travel

The French hold the world rail speed record, more than 300 miles per hour, logged by their space-age service, *train à grande vitesse* (TGV, tay jay vay). For comfort, efficiency, and cleanliness, the government-operated rail system, both express and local, is hard to beat. Normal TGV speeds are in the 150-200 mile per hour range, and the sound of the fast-flicking utility poles passing by your window is no more than a whisper. Sometimes a TGV train can pass through a station at more than 150 miles an hour, only 50 yards from where you are standing, and you won't be aware of it.

The TGV has even put some airline routes out of business. For example, since the opening of the channel tunnel, you can travel between Paris and London faster by rail than by air. There is a surcharge for riding the TGV, and you need a reservation and seat assignment, available at all major stations.

Because the rail system is so good, it's hardly worth considering buses or airplanes for going from place to place within the country. It's also so fast that it isn't usually worth buying a sleeping berth.

If you plan to do extensive train traveling in addition to cycling, you might consider carrying a City-to-City timetable. It's about the size of a paperback and can be a useful reference. Write: Bureau de Vente des Documents, Tarifares, 212 Rue de Bercy, Paris 75571 or ask at ticket offices in Paris. In French it is called *Horaire Ville à Ville* (or air veel ah veel).

French train stations can be confusing to Americans, particularly those not familiar even with American stations. If you don't pay close attention it's easy to find yourself on the wrong train. However, there are many places to check to avoid unwanted mistakes: the main departure board in the station concourse, the electronic boards on each platform, the sign boards on the car, the conductor, and your fellow passengers.

Be careful; you may have the right platform, the right train, and still be wrong. If you are on the wrong car and it gets separated somewhere down the line, you could end up in Clermont-Ferrand when you wanted to go to Lyon. Also you may get on a train that came in at exactly the time it was supposed to. But that doesn't make it your train.

Each car has signs giving its final destination and its number. Somewhere near the center of the platform, a display shows the makeup of each train using that platform. By checking it you can position yourself where your assigned car will stop. While waiting for your train, stand away from the tracks, well behind the yellow line. Through trains go by with frightening speed.

French rail tickets come in two classes, first and second. First class is about 50 percent more expensive and not worth the extra cost on short runs. Nor is there an advantage in buying a round-trip ticket. Kids under 4 ride free; 4 to 11, half price.

If you are 60 or older, a bargain is available—*Carte Vermeil* (pronounced cart ver may eh). For Fr 165 (about $35) it entitles you to travel at half-fare on any rail line, as long as it isn't at peak periods. These can be bought at any rail station or at the SNCF, the French abbreviation for the National Rail Service (Societé National de Chemin de Fer) desks at Paris airports.

The French railroads have a similar discount program for students. It is called *Carrismo* and offers four trips for Fr 190 (about $38) or eight trips at Fr 390 (about $78) at off-peak periods. The maximum age is 25; check at any rail station.

You can avoid wasting time in ticket lines by buying a ticket from an automated ticket machine, a *billeterie*. It's not as daunting as it looks. If your destination appears on the list posted on the machine, enter its corresponding number. When it asks if you want first or second class, enter A or B, respectively. Enter O for normal tariff, and the ticket price will appear. Add the coins necessary, and *Voila!* Your ticket will pop out.

If you need sleeper accommodations, you will need to deal with a clerk. There are some choices. In first class, private compartments are available, as well as compartments of four. Berth price is the same whether you are traveling first or second class, about $18 per person. You normally need to reserve at least two hours in advance of departure, but a conductor will help you if he has space available, even as the train is about to depart.

In second class, sleeping is arranged six berths, *couchettes* (kou shet), to a compartment. The compartments are co-ed, and it's a bit more intimacy than many Americans enjoy. Travelers remove only their shoes, and keep their valuables under tight control. If they feel uncomfortable with the situation, women traveling alone can ask the conductor for a change of berth.

Finding your berth assignment in the dark on a moving train can be a challenge. It's best to board at point of origination before they turn the lights off. It's a good idea to have an alarm clock if you have an intermediate destination. It's also wise to carry some food with you, as food service is often expensive or nonexistent.

After you have bought your ticket (you can pay with a credit card) it's necessary to validate it, in French, *compostez* (kahm post ay). If you forget, the conductor may fine you on the spot, but he usually won't. Waist-high composting machines, usually orange, stand guard between the station and the tracks. Simply slip your ticket into the slot of the machine and it will be date-stamped. Tickets are also available from the conductor, but there is a substantial surcharge.

In Paris there are six different rail stations called *gares* (gahr). They and the regions they serve are:

Gare de Montparnasse	Brittany and west coast
Gare de Lyon	Burgundy and south of France
Gare d'Austerlitz	The Midi and the southwest
Gare de l'Est	Eastern part of the country
Gare du Nord	English channel area, boat trains from Dunkerque, Boulogne, and Calais

Gare St. Lazare   Normandy, Rouen, and boat trains
                                     from Dieppe, Le Havre, Cherbourg

Metropolitan stations provide shower facilities for travelers. Entrance to shower/rest rooms will often be co-ed, presided over by a large female, who will sell you an entry ticket, the cost of which will depend on the purpose of your visit. It's a good idea to be equipped with small change in case access is coin-operated. Large stations also offer a tourist information office. In Paris you can also call the railroad's English-speaking information office at (1) 45 82 08 41.

Train stations pose a special problem for cyclists: How to handle the stairways? For going down, just stand your bike up on its back wheel and let it bounce down vertically holding on to the handle bars. There's no easy way for getting it back up.

Trees provide beauty, shade, and a welcome windbreak for the cyclist along the canals. Gravel trails such as this one make a reasonable surface for cycling.

Buses

Where the trains don't go, you can almost always find a local or regional bus that does. Some take bikes.

Getting Around by Car

Be careful; while the French drive on the right like Americans, they have a few rules and habits that you should know about. At an intersection in France, the person approaching you from your right has the right of way. This is true in the United States, but not nearly to the same extent. In France, cars coming out of small roads to your right can quite legally cut you off. The exception is if the road you are on displays a yellow diamond. This indicates you are on a through highway and have the right of way.

Be especially careful on city streets and traffic rotaries: the guy on the right can legally cut in front of you, and frequently will.

This rule is particularly in force on the *Etoile*, the frightening circle around Paris' *Arc de Triomphe*, where converging traffic from a dozen streets sorts itself out following that rule and without benefit of traffic lights or traffic cops. An expatriate American housewife reported that she went around the monument 10 times before she could screw up the courage to make the move to get off.

French drivers are expert, but they are incurable sociopaths. They seem to have a compulsion to get as close as they can to your rear bumper, unnerving to many Americans.

Speed limits: limited access superhighways, 130 kilometers per hour (80 miles per hour); dual highways, 110 kilometers per hour (68 miles per hour); other highways outside of built-up areas, 90 kilometers per hour (56 miles per hour).

In towns and cities, parking is a major problem, but parking garages and lots can be found by following prominent "P" signs. Curbside parking is usually metered. If you can find a parking space, look nearby for an *horodateur* (oar ah dah tour), a machine that with a few coins will issue a slip to put inside your windshield, good for the amount of parking time you have bought. In some particularly narrow streets, cars park straddling the curb. Follow the local custom.

Many French country roads consist of two traffic lanes without suitable shoulders for bicycles. Theoretically, the bicyclist has the right of way. If you are following bikes, wait for oncoming traffic to clear, put on your left turn signal, then pull out to pass.

Glossary

Some phrases and terms dealing with transportation:

Gare	gahr	Railroad station
Guichet	gwee shay	Ticket window
Billet	bee yay	Ticket

Voie	vwah	Track
Quai	kay	Platform
Compostez votre billet	kahm post ay bee yay	Validate your vote ticket by getting it stamped before boarding. You can be fined if you don't *compostez.*
Train à grande vitesse (TGV)	tay jay vay	Fastest train service. Surcharge and reservation required.
Salle d'attente	sahl da tahnt	Waiting room
Première ou deuxième classe?	pree miairou dooz ee em klahs	Do you want first or second class?
Allez et retour	ahl ay ay ray tour	Round trip
Autocar	auto car	Bus
Camion	kah mi yon	Truck
Voiture	vwah tyur	Automobile
Vélo, bicyclette	vay low, bee see kleht	Bicycle
VTT	vay tay tay	Mountain bike
Vélo moteur	vay low mo tour	Motorbike
Moto	moh toh	Motorbike
Vitesse	vee tess	Speed
Peniche	pen eesh	Canal barge
Bateau moteur	baht oh mo tour	Motorboat
Bateau à voile	baht oh ah vwahl	Sailboat
Consigne	kahn seen	Parcel rooms or coin parcel boxes in stations
Couchette	kou shet	Bunk in compartment
Wagon lit	vah gon lee	Sleeping car
Sortie	sor tee	Way out, exit

Chapter 8

Staying Healthy and in Touch

Staying Healthy

You and your companion are pedaling down the towpath out in France's backcountry when your friend loses control and runs into a tree. He needs medical attention. What can you do?

If it's serious, find the nearest person and yell "Help!" In French, it's "*M'aidez!*" pronounced "MAY DAY." Good, qualified doctors and emergency services are thick on the ground in France and if they know they are needed, you can count on quick and professional reaction. In France, 15 on the telephone is the equivalent of our 911 for emergencies.

The maps in this book show you the communities that have hospitals along the routes. Most first aid problems will be handled free at hospital emergency rooms, *le service des urgences*.

In addition, pharmacists are not only qualified, but obliged to render first aid if asked, and all villages large enough to have stores will have a pharmacy. Look for the sign with the green cross; if your problem happens after closing hours, pharmacies take turns being on call. The police will know which one has the duty.

If you have a serious health problem in a hotel or guest house, you should know that in France, doctors make house calls. You can ask your host to call one.

Dog bites can be dangerous. You should seek immediate medical advice against rabies. Remember where it occurred and a description of the dog. Snakes in France are not a problem; there are only two types of poisonous ones, and they are rarely seen.

If you are in the mood for a swim, try to make sure that the water is not contaminated. If you are swimming in the ocean, be mindful that there can be strong undertows and riptides, especially in Brittany. Red flags flying at beaches mean stay out of the water.

49

In Redon in Brittany, the cobbled street in front of a popular bakery is a social meeting place.

Postal Services

If receiving mail is important, it's a good idea when planning your itinerary to select a few towns as general delivery mail drops. Instruct your correspondents to send mail to you at the named towns within specified dates. They should allow two weeks for its arrival before your scheduled pick-up date. You should be addressed, last name first, "*c/o Poste Restante.*" They should use your official name as it appears on your passport, not nicknames. They should also place the ZIP number in front of the name of the city or town.

If the town has more than one post office, *poste restante* will be held at the main office. Be sure you have your passport with you. There may be a small fee.

If the post office is closed, you can buy stamps at kiosks and tobacconists, *tabacs*. Be sure that all of your outgoing mail is marked for air, *par avion*, or it may end up on a slow ship.

American Express will also hold mail for you in the cities where they have that service. There is a per-piece charge.

In addition to stamps, some post offices can provide you credit card cash advances. They can also provide shipping boxes and telephone assistance. Telephone books for all of France are available at all post offices.

Canadians can use Canadian missions as mail drops, but for letter mail only, no forwarding services. Mail must be picked up in person. For a list of Canadian consulates in France, see Chapter 11.

Telephones

French telephones can be a challenge to Americans because the sounds are different, but the system is highly sophisticated and reliable, once you understand its workings. Pay telephones increasingly accept special cards, *telecartes*, in the slot. You can buy them in 50- and 120-franc units in post offices, tobacco shops, kiosks.

To operate pay phones: remove the handset and insert your *telecarte* in the slot. The number of calling units remaining on your card will be shown on a small screen. Dial your number, and when your call is finished you will note on the screen the number of calling units remaining.

If you need "information" to find a number within France, dial 12. For international inquiries, dial 19-33, plus the country code.

French telephone numbers have eight digits, and to call anyone in France, you simply dial the eight-digit number, with an important exception—the Paris region. To call Paris from the rest of the country, dial 16 plus 1 plus the eight-digit number. To call the rest of the country from Paris, dial 16 plus the eight digit number. No prefixes are required for calls made and received within the Paris metropolitan area.

Toll calls are half-price from 10:30 P.M. to 8 A.M. weekdays and on weekends.

Glossary

An explanation of some French terms you may encounter:

Médicin, docteur	meh deh sen	Doctor
Infirmière	ahn fairm ee yair	Nurse
M'aidez!	may day	Help!
Pharmacie	farm ah see	Pharmacy
Pharmacien	farm ah see eh	Druggist
Ordonnance	or do nahnce	Prescription
Service des urgences	sairvees dayz urjahnts	Emergency squad
Gendarmes	jahn darm	National police force
Gendarmarie	jahn darm ar ee	police station
Pompiers	pohmp ee yea	Firemen
Hôpital	hoh pee tahl	Hospital
Clinique	klineek	clinic
Poste restante	post res tahnt	General delivery
Timbre poste	tom breh post	Postage stamp
Bureau de Poste (PTT)	byou roh deh post (pay tay tay)	Post office
Caisse	kess	Cashier
Allo	ah loh	Hello
Renseignement	ron sen moh	Information
Occupé	oh cou pay	Busy signal
Minitel	min ee tel	Small computer furnished free to phone subscribers in place of phone books.

Chapter 9

Dealing with Language, Manners, and Customs

"I stayed in Paris for a weekend and I couldn't wait to get out. The people are rude." You may have heard this common litany and its source is nearly always a first-time traveler who wonders why the French don't seem to know what he or she is talking about.

Rudeness is not a French characteristic. If you don't believe it, live for a while in a French community, where not only will the shopkeeper always greet you politely, but so will his customers, whether or not they know you.

Why the bad reputation? Language is the problem. The French, unlike most Europeans, are not linguists. They believe that the French language is the most beautiful in the world, and spend no more time trying to be fluent in English than the average American does learning French. Parisians become inured to Americans racing to catch planes, trying to find a charming hotel for under 100 francs, or wondering why the banks are closed at noon. Neither can understand the other. Translation: rudeness.

Turn the tables and imagine an unsophisticated Frenchman getting off the plane at Kennedy Airport. He knows no English, doesn't understand how to get into Manhattan, and can't make himself understood by the cab driver who, himself, just arrived from Odessa and hasn't a clue where Manhattan is either.

The hectic pace of big cities like Paris and New York also tends to increase the rudeness quotient. Once you are able to get to the quiet eddies, however, even in Paris, you will find that courtesy and helpfulness are as common as anywhere in the world.

Having people traveling with you who have some knowledge of French is a big help, but it's not vital for a happy tour. If, in your schooling, you had some high school French, find a phrase book and do some reviewing. The French are pleased when foreigners try to speak their language; it's a compliment.

You'll do best if you forget your fears of being wrong, or of mispronouncing; just stick your neck out and jump in. Self-confidence is a big plus to learning a new language. The Frenchman may not understand what you are saying, but he won't laugh at you.

You'll find there are many French words that look familiar. And many American words are a part of the modern French language. Some words we share: camping, jogging, parking, hamburgers, picnic, stop, whiskey, sandwich, menu.

Here is a linguistic trick that can come in handy. When you can't think of the French word, think of the English word; come up with an obscure synonym for it and give it a French pronunciation. It may save the day for you. For example: somebody remarks to you about the weather. You want to be polite, but can't think of the French word for "perfect." An English synonym is "imPECCable." Reply in your best French, *impeccahble*. Suddenly you are a worldly and courteous linguist.

Some other words you think you don't know, but you do: in English, serious; in French, *grave* (grahve). In English, begin; in French, *commence* (commahnce). In English, large; in French, *grand* (grahnd).

A good way to help memorize words and phrases is with flash cards. Cut up index cards into smaller blank cards. Put the English word or phrase on one side, the equivalent in French on the other. Flick through the stack during coffee breaks, TV commercial breaks, or while riding to work. You'll be surprised how fast you can build a useful vocabulary.

Communications can sometimes be tricky. Be careful of the clerk who nods vigorously that he or she knows exactly what it is you want. People don't like to disappoint and nodding "Yes," even when they don't understand, is sometimes easier.

In hotels you'll seldom have a serious language problem— as long as the conversation remains on a familiar subject. Hotel clerks know about double and single beds, toilets, bathtubs, and what to respond when you ask when breakfast is served. They may fail completely when you ask the condition of the towpath for the next 30 miles.

When you are looking for someone who speaks English, forget the question you learned from your phrase book: "Parlez-vous anglais?" Just say, "Do you speak English?" The response will answer the question.

The French make it a bit easier for nonlinguistic Americans than we do for visiting French. Almost any town of any size has a tourist office and most employees will understand you. Look for signs bearing a large "I" or that say *Syndicate d'Initiative* or *Office de Tourisme*.

They can give invaluable help in many ways: where to find services, opening hours of shops and museums, where you can find a good *cassoulet* or *boeuf bourguignon*, and even more important, a room within your budget. There is no charge for their help, except perhaps a reimbursement for phone calls. Usually there is a plate for tips.

Before starting off in the morning, you may be able to lighten your load by finding a taxi driver who will take your packs and those of your companions to your next hotel, guest house, or campground for a reasonable charge. Be sure the bags are well marked and that they are expected at the other end. Your hotel clerk may be able to help in the negotiation.

French roads are almost always well marked. Hamlets and villages are all identified, not only by a sign at the entrance, but also at the exit, a similar sign with a line through it. It tells you where you were.

A helpful profusion of signs also tells you the direction of other villages and hamlets, and even of specific farms, most of which bear names. There is a small glitch in the system. Where one highway joins another for a stretch, it may lose its identity until it takes off again on its own. The system leaves it to the user to guess in which direction to go. City streets, too, change names frequently.

In France highway route numbers are mnemonic. The prefix "A" means that it is an *autoroute*, a high-speed superhighway, usually a toll road. Cyclists are not welcome. The prefix "N" designates a major intercity highway, usually two or three lanes and thick with trucks. Cyclists should avoid them, too. Those prefixed "C" and "D" are less-traveled country highways. Wherever possible stick to these.

A mechanical problem may occur on your route. A bicycle repair shop may not be handy. Try to find an auto mechanic or a machine shop. Ask where you can find a *garagiste* or a *mécanicien*. The French have grown up with bicycles; there is little that is mysterious about them, and usually any qualified mechanic can provide at least temporary repairs to get you moving again. And don't be surprised if when you ask "how much?" he shrugs his shoulders and answers, "Rien," nothing.

If you need a bank during the noon hour, forget it. Most banks are open from 9 A.M. until noon, then from 2 until 4 P.M. If you want to change money, it's best to check around for the best rate. Hotels, airports, restaurants, and tourist offices usually offer the worst terms.

Noon closings are sacrosanct in France, except in the largest cities, where larger stores may remain open. Shops normally stay open until 6 or 7 P.M. The closer to the south, the longer the noon closing period and the later the closing time. Museums are usually closed on Tuesdays while some shops are closed Mondays.

Tipping

While most restaurants and hotel dining rooms indicate on their menus *service compris*, tip included, most people leave their small change behind. Here are some guideposts for tipping for other services rendered:

Taxis and hairdressers	10 percent
Theater ushers	Fr 1–2
Coat checkers	Fr 5
Washroom attendants	Fr 5
Chambermaids	Fr 10 per day if stay is longer than three days
Porters	Fr 10 per item
Guides	Fr 5–10

Governmental Differences

In France, most vital public services, including utilities, telephone service, railroad—even Air France—are government owned and operated.

The major divisions of the country are *départments*, each about the size of a large county. The departmental capital is called a *préfecture*.

While larger towns and cities have municipal police, the *gendarmes*, who are under army control, have overall national police responsibility. There is a *gendarmarie*, barracks, in all major towns.

National Holidays

In France, everything except bars and restaurants will be closed on these days:

January 1	New Year's Day
Easter Monday	
May 1	May Day
May 8	V-E Day
July 14	Bastille Day
August 15	Assumption Day
November 1	All Saints Day
November 11	Armistice Day
December 25	Christmas

Rules for Walking

As a rule you can walk—or ride—almost anywhere you want to in France. But remember these rules:

- Don't leave gates open
- Don't trample crops
- Don't litter
- Don't bother farm animals or wildlife
- Be sure fires are out
- Make no excessive noise
- Don't help yourself to fruit or vegetables, or even mushrooms in the forest. It's considered stealing.

Finding a Toilet

Your best bet is to use those of a good bar or restaurant, usually the newer the more satisfactory. From your canalside route, look for a church steeple. *Cafés* and bars can almost always be found within its shadow. But it is never good form to use these facilities without buying at least a soft drink before leaving.

Public toilets, unless attended, tend to be less satisfactory. Look for signs, *toilettes* or *W.C.* (water closet) pronounced "vay say."

Along the canals you can often find public toilets at village canal ports, marinas, or campgrounds.

The battlement of Carcassonne in Midi is one of France's most popular tourist destinations. The canal path passes through the center of the modern city.

Chapter 10

Signs Along the Way

Here is an explanation of road signs, canal signs, and trail signs that you will probably encounter.

Note: signs giving distance are all in kilometers, not miles. To convert, divide kilometers in half and add about 10 percent. Not all signs need be believed. In Josselin in Brittany the sign on a restaurant said: *"Ouvert à toutes heures"* (always open). It was closed.

Deviation	day vee ah sion	Detour
Inondée, inondation	ee non day, ee non dah sion	Flooding ahead, usually in the early spring
Verglas frequent	vair glah free kwent	Danger of black ice on highway in winter
Ecluse	ay klouz	Canal lock
Eclusier	ay klouz ee ay	Lockkeeper (male)
Eclusière	ay klouz ee air	Lockkeeper (female)
Chemin d'halage	sheh meh dah lahj	Canal towpath
Rue	rou	Street
Boulevard,	boo lay var	Street
Avenue	ah ven new	Street
Randonée, sentier	rahn doh nay, sahn tee yay	Trail for hiking or cycling
Autoroute	auto route	Limited access super highway, usually tollway
Mairie or Hôtel de Ville	may ree, oh tel de veel	Town hall, city hall

Château/manoir	shah tow, man wahr	Large estate
Moulin	moo lahn	Mill
Toutes (or autres) directions	toot, (oh treh) dee rek sion	The way out of town (with arrow)
Interdit or defense d'entrer	in tare dee, day fahns dahn tray	Prohibited to enter or stay out
Ville, village	veel, veel ahj	City, village
Hameau	hahmoh	Hamlet
Commune	ko myoun	Neighborhood
Sauf riverains	sohf ree vrain	Traffic is restricted to residents
Marché lundi	marsh ay loon dee	Monday is market day
A Vendre	ah vahn dreh,	For sale
A Lour	ah lou ay	For rent
Promotion	proh moh sion	On sale
Jumelée avec—	jou mel ay ah vek—	The community is twinned with a city in another country for social and cultural intercourse
Chien méchant	she ehn may shant	Beware of dog
Gratuit	graht twee	Free
Eglise	ay gleese	Church
Sortie	sor tee	Exit
A Pied	ah pee eh	On foot
A Cheval	ah shev ahl	On horseback
Carrefour	kar ef our	Crossroads
Piste cyclable	peest see klahb	Improved roadway made especially for bicyclists
Hôtel de canine	oh tel de ka neen	Dog kennel
Quick	kweek	A McDonald's with a French accent
Poubelle	pou bell	Trash can
Laverie automatique	lahvairee auto ma teek	Coin-operated Laundry

Chapter 11

Questions and Answers

Q–*What do you do about laundry?*
A–Most touring cyclists take care of their laundry at the same time they are bathing themselves. Wash out the underwear, shirts, and socks you just took off in the tub or shower. If they are fast drying, they'll be ready to wear or pack the next morning. In larger towns you can often find coin-operated laundries, *laveries*. Ask at the tourist office.

Q–*Dickering for a better price—is it done?*
A–In most shops, no. Small hotels and antique shops, yes; sometimes successfully.

Q–*What can you do if you feel you are being cheated by a taxi driver or shopkeeper?*
A–Call a policeman. The French government is protective of foreign tourists, and even the threat of a policeman on the scene may change things.

Q–*What do you do if your passport is missing?*
A–Contact the U.S. Embassy in Paris or U.S. Consulates in:

Paris	2 Avenue Gabriel
	Tel. (33) (1) 43-12-22-22
Bordeaux	22 Cours du Marechal Foch
	Tel. (33) 56-52-65-95
Marseilles	12 Boulevard Paul Peytral
	Tel. (33) 91-54-92-00
Strasbourg	15 Avenue d'Alsace
	Tel. (33) 88-35-31-04

Canadians should contact any of these Canadian consulates:

Paris	35 Montaigne Avenue
	Tel. (33) (1) 44 43 29 00
Lyon	74 de Bonnel St., 3rd floor
	Tel. (33) 72 61 15 25
Nice	64, Avenue Jean Medicin

Tel. (33) (1) 93 92 93 22
Strasbourg Rue de Riad, La Watzenau
Tel. (33) 88 96 65 02
Toulouse 30 Strasbourg Boulevard
Tel. (33) 61 99 30 16

Q–*Someone in your group has a medical emergency—what do you do?*
A–Seek help at the nearest fire house, doctor's office, pharmacy, hospital, police station, town hall, tourist office, or dial 15, which is similar to 911. When none of the above is handy, yell, "MAY DAY!" It's French for "HELP!"

Q–*Your glasses need repair; what do you do?*
A–Just as you would at home, you find an optician; it's the same in French. Most repairs will be free, *gratuit.*

Q–*How much stuff can I bring back into the United States duty-free?*
A–Up to $400 per person. Family members can pool their allowance. There is no duty on antiques more than 100 years old, and there are special limitations on alcohol, cigars, and perfume. Write: U.S. Customs Service, 1301 Constitution Ave., Washington, DC 20229 for booklet "Know Before You Go."

Q–*What can Canadians bring back?*
A–Everything acquired must be declared, and it's a good idea to keep all receipts. If you have been abroad for seven days or longer, you have a $500 (Canadian) exemption per person. Restricted items include meat and milk products, weapons, vehicles, plants, exotic animals, obscene materials, hate propaganda, and goods harmful to the environment. For more information: 800-461-9999 within Canada; 613-993-0534 from outside Canada. Open 24 hours per day.

Q–*How difficult is it to get around Paris by public transportation?*
A–The Paris subway system, the *métro,* may be the most consumer-friendly system in the world. You need no knowledge of French, just an ability to read the easy graphics of the maps and you can reach any part of this magnificent city.

Q–*What is the story on "duty-free" shops?*
A–Well-advertised airport duty-free shops save you no duty at all. What they don't charge is the French value-added tax. As a transient foreigner, you are exempt from VAT anyway, if you apply for a refund within 30 days of purchase.

Q–*How do you go about getting your VAT refund?*
A–Normally, the store that sells you a large ticket item can take care of the forms and send them on to the French government. In due course, you will receive a check. The problem is that the check will come in French francs, which may cause problems at small, unsophisticated banks. Conversion of these checks can be handled by contacting Ruesch, International, 700 11th Street NW, Washington, DC 20001-4507.

Chapter 12

Some Background on Brittany

How to Get There and Back

The start point for the tour along the Canal Nantes à Brest is the canal/river crossroads village of Pontivy. Most direct route is from Paris (Gare Montparnasse) to the regional capital of Rennes, about two hours. Change at Rennes to the regional TER train service that serves Pontivy (one hour). It is also possible to travel from Rennes to Pontivy by bus (autocar) via Redon and Vannes.

Returning to civilization after your tour is ended at Nantes is quick and easy. There is frequent, fast, and comfortable TGV nonstop service direct to Paris (about 2 1/2 hours).

Maritime, Celtic, and provincial. Brittany, pointing like a gnarled thumb into the Atlantic at France's extreme northwest, has always been one of its most nonconformist regions. Its people with their Celtic ancestry give it a closer relationship to Cornwall, Wales, and Ireland than to the rest of France. Its ancient language, traditions, costumes, architecture, and culinary specialties make Brittany a highly distinctive gem. Add to this a wondrously jagged coastline, boiling sea, red rock cliffs, and its pastoral, often unspoiled and tourist-less interior. Who needs more excuse to explore it?

Some of the finest beaches in France are in Brittany, but watch out for the tides: at Mont St. Michel they are among the highest in the world—up to 48 feet at times. This makes the present shoreline and the place on the beach where you left your boat 6 hours before as much as 12 miles apart. Wild about archaeology? The remnants of early man in Brittany are older and as dense as in any other region of the world.

Through the Interior

Brittany is loaded with rose-covered inns and village streets where the 400-year-old overhanging houses almost meet over

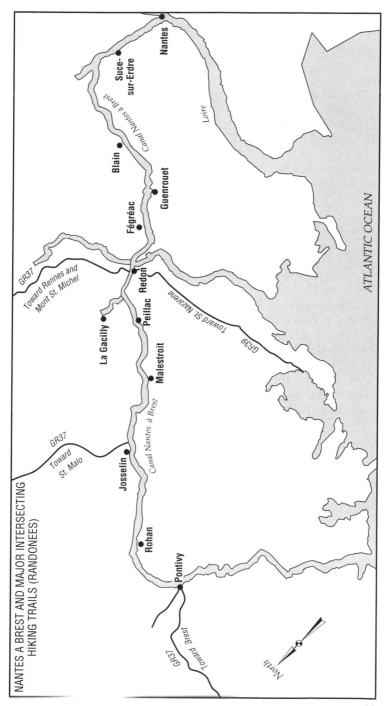

NANTES A BREST AND MAJOR INTERSECTING HIKING TRAILS (RANDONEES)

the cobblestone streets. Out in the countryside, whitewashed cottages with slate roofs surrounded by stone walls sit amidst small green meadows dotted with cows and sheep.

Your cycling route will take you 128 easy miles through the center of what is called the *Argoat*, the lush interior. You will be following a section of the Canal Nantes à Brest, riding its original gravel towpaths. A century and a half ago, these paths were thick with the hoof marks of oxen and dray horses, motive power for the barges using this inland route.

To a large extent you and the canal will share valleys with the river that carved it. Often there will be only the song of your tires on the gravel, the sounds of the birds in the trees, and the splash of a startled fish or swan. There are cities at each end, Pontivy and Nantes, but in between are long stretches of quiet riding, punctuated here and there by small, charming Breton towns and villages.

Inland Brittany is mostly plains and low hills. Compared with the rest of France, Brittany is densely cultivated, but the farms are small, often less than 25 acres. Many are bordered by dry stone walls made of slabs held together by chestnut branches. Your route will pass through oak and beech forests, which once covered the entire land.

As you travel through the countryside, the place names reflect the country's Celtic cultural origins and sound like places in no other area of France. Those that begin "Ploe," "Plou," or "Plo" refer to parish. A common prefix is "Ker," which means village or house and is also often the first syllable of a Breton family name. "Loc" means holy place and "Tre" or "Tref" is a parish subdivision. "Lann" means church.

History

For Brittany it starts about 3,500 years before Christ, when its mysterious earliest inhabitants made careers of moving around huge stones called *megaliths* and arranging them in curious patterns. Some time after 500 B.C., the Celts arrived on the scene, later to be subjugated by the Romans about 50 years before the birth of Christ. Those who decided not to hang in sailed the narrow English Channel and their natural fecundity spread their seed as far as Ireland.

When the hordes from the East overcame the Roman Empire, including what is now England, about 350 A.D., some of the Celts there decided their former land of Brittany was safer. They did a reverse migration to get away from the threatening Anglo-Saxons, and named their new nation Armor or Armorica, which means "little Britain."

The language connection to Wales, Cornwall, and Ireland dates to the return of the Celts. For centuries thereafter the Breton language was the official tongue. But for the last-ditch efforts of linguistic die-hards, the language would have disappeared entirely. Today French is the *lingua franca* and Breton is heard only in remote areas of Lower Brittany, the westernmost half of the region.

Breton history has it that after the death of Christ, one of his apostles, Joseph of Arimathea, carried one of the cups with a few drops of divine blood from the Last Supper to what is now Brittany. Subsequently, the story goes, he lived for many years in the Forest of Paimpont in Brittany, then vanished. In the sixth century, King Arthur with 50 knights set out from England in search of the cup, the Holy Grail, which legend tells us, could only be found by one of pure heart. (If you qualify, keep your eyes open as you cycle through this ancient land.)

The ninth century was the high-water mark for Armor, or Brittany, as a nation; in 1532 the duchy of Brittany became a part of France.

Churches

As in the rest of France, churches in Brittany are thick on the ground, but because prosperity arrived only recently, don't expect them to have the richness found elsewhere. Every hamlet has at least a chapel, but in the smaller communities many of the churches today are used only on local saint's days. Many of them were built before the sixteenth century, and usually these are rectangular in shape. Later churches followed the Latin cross design.

Brittany has more than its share of saints, many of whom are regional, with no official papal standing. One of the most popular is Saint Yves, the righter of wrongs and patron saint of lawyers, canonized in 1347. Saint Anne, patron of mothers, is another high on the regional hit parade.

If your schedule permits, try to arrange to be where the locals are celebrating a *pardon*, a uniquely Breton religious festival. It's your best opportunity to observe one of the most important examples of Breton's ancient culture. From the back of old Breton wardrobes come heirlooms from centuries past, including ladies' headdresses a foot and a half tall, old lace and velvet collars, and colorful aprons. Picturesque processions start in the afternoon. Everyone parades with candles, banners, and statues of saints. Before the day is over the festivities often include hymn singing, dancing, and even wrestling.

Pardons are held in a number of towns at specific dates. The one closest to your canalside route is held at Josselin each September 8.

Castles and Châteaux

Ancient residences of nobility and aristocracy, fortified and unfortified, dot the Breton landscape and your route will bring

The inland harbor at Redon. These ancient warehouses served a prosperous salt trade. From here navigable waterways reach out in all four directions.

you close to many. Some of the finest examples have been reconstructed and refurnished and opened to the public. Many house specialty museums. Some are still owned by the original families, and to help pay the taxes have been turned into up-market inns or private schools. Some are still used as they were designed centuries ago—to be the home of the wealthy owner. Groves of old pines behind high stone walls may hide a romantic old *château* or manor house, but there's no law against peeking behind them for a glimpse of a moat or turret as you pass by.

Towns

Almost every Breton village and town is living history. Town centers are where you'll find things pretty much as they were 400 to 500 years ago. Breton townsmen think nothing of living in a house built in the fifteenth century. Currently there is a nationwide movement to protect these old town centers from the encroachment of progress and the automobile. In many towns regional governments subsidize the rebuilding of ancient houses. Often the most picturesque streets have been blocked off and pedestrianized, making delightful shopping arcades far more attractive than modern malls. You will usually find the best selection of restaurants in the old town centers.

The Seasons

Spring is mild and flower-scented. There are frequent showers. Sometimes if the winter has been particularly wet, flooding may cause problems for riders along the low-lying canals. When the sun is out spring in Brittany can be unbeatable, especially along the waterways where nature is at its best. Wildflowers, particularly gorse and broom, are everywhere.

From June to September, city-bound Frenchmen and their families make for Brittany, but mostly for the coastal beaches. From mid-July to mid-August you will need a reservation if you want a bed. Inland, however, the problem is not so grave. Don't expect the towpaths to be crowded even in mid-summer, but you should still phone ahead for accommodations. Even in summer, showers will keep the fields green, and the ocean breezes will keep you from sunstroke. Mean temperature: 62 degrees F.

By mid-October natives start looking for gales from the northeast and northwest, with frequent low pressure systems bringing extended rainy periods. While winter is a time when Bretons live behind closed shutters, Brittany's winters by most standards are mild with only occasional bitterness, usually coming from the east.

Food and Drink

In cuisine, Brittany doesn't take a back seat to any other region of France. The Breton specialty is seafood and fish, not surprising when no place is farther than 40 miles from saltwater. If you encounter *lobster armoricaine* don't expect a New England dinner that the chef misspelled. It's a Breton specialty featuring lobster in a hot sauce called *coulis*. You might also want to try the Breton version of bouillabaisse, a fish soup called *cotriade*. Around Nantes eels are a specialty.

You are in one of the prime market growing areas of France, and while the average farm is small, the region supplies the entire country with a third of its vegetables and half of its eggs and poultry. Particularly notable are pork, mutton, artichokes, and apples. As in Normandy, look for crêperies, often only simple booths facing the sidewalk and featuring a puzzling variety of pancakes, crêpes, and galettes, with condiments: yogurt, jam, cheese, or ham. The cost is moderate and crêpes make a great meal for eating on the fly.

The local drink is cider, mildly alcoholic. The only Breton wine is *muscadet*, a dry, white, fruity wine made from grapes grown in the Nantes area.

Industry

Fishing continues to be a major industry for Bretons as it has for centuries. They contribute one-third of all the fish consumed in France. The catch includes sole, mullet, turbot, skate, bass, sea bream, mackerel, and sardines. Deep sea catches include tuna and cod. Oyster cultivation is centered around Morbihan on the Biscay and Concale on the channel coast.

Another resource of the sea is marine fertilizer made from algae and seaweed, used traditionally in their natural state or refined into a powder.

Brittany is not heavily industrialized but half of all ships built in France are built here. St. Nazaire is a major producer of supertankers. The largest employers are the military arsenals at Lorient and Brest. Other industries: canning, tin mining, and granite quarrying.

Two Suggested Detours

Because the sea is so much a part of Brittany, you shouldn't leave without at least a taste of salt. Here are two suggested detours: one toward the Channel Coast to visit St. Malo and Mont St. Michel, and the other south toward the Golfe du Morbihan and the beaches and megaliths of Carnac. Both can be reached by rail from Redon, a midway point on your canal route, with or without your bicycle.

St. Malo, together with Mont St. Michel, is one of France's premier tourist spots. Called the Emerald Coast, this area was an ancient lair of pirates. St. Malo is an old port with remarkably preserved ramparts. Off to the east, 32 miles down the coast, is the magic of Mont St. Michel, whose likeness has probably adorned more calendars than the Matterhorn or Yosemite Falls. It is a tight formation of Gothic towers, spires, and pinnacles that, when the tide is in, seems to rise sharply out of the sea. When the tide is out, it stands like a beached ship against the endless tidal flats.

Morbihan is a complex seascape of peninsulas, bays, tidal flats, and estuaries southwest of Redon on the Bay of Biscay. In season it is lively with thousands of tourists who come for the fishing, sailing, and swimming. Its beaches are superb. On the far side of the gulf is Carnac, where more than 3,000 mysterious standing stones or *menhirs* litter the countryside and get in the way of road builders and developers. Some of them weigh up to 350 tons and are up to 20 feet high. Some are single sentinels; some are arranged by the hundreds in puzzling military-like formations.

You will note that coastal life is closely related to the rhythm of the sea, the diurnal tides. The sea is clean and most beautiful at high tide, but low tide is when you can catch your dinner. Away from cultivated seafood areas you can try for clams, mussels, cockles, and crabs without need for a license.

Be careful if you are swimming on unguarded beaches. The Atlantic creates dangerous undertows and currents. If a red flag is flying, swimming is unsafe. Head for the showers.

Chapter 13

About the Canal You'll Be Following

The canal that will be your constant companion for the next few days was built under the stewardship of Napoleon in the early part of the nineteenth century to provide a dependable inland link between Brest and Nantes, two of France's most important Atlantic seaports. The canal runs generally southeast, parallel to Brittany's Atlantic coast. The designers canalized existing rivers where possible and crossed watersheds independently where necessary.

In its original form, the canal gave barge traffic, including vital military supplies, a 224-mile inland route with immunity from Atlantic storms, and even more importantly, from unfriendly navies. For more than a century, it formed an important part of France's highly developed inland waterway system.

With the decline of commercial barge traffic in the second quarter of this century, the Canal Nantes à Brest was allowed to fall into disrepair. The section west of Pontivy remains out of service, but with sharply increasing usage by pleasure boats in recent years, politicians are again appreciating the canal's importance to the regional economy. Within the past four or five years, the entire length from Pontivy to Nantes has been dredged, and the locks have been refurbished.

In some areas the paths, too, suffered from neglect. However, lockkeepers use the paths to move from one lock to another, and with heavier canal usage, path condition also improved. Increased waterway traffic alone will continue to improve the towpath for cyclists in the future, simply through increased use.

At the outset the canal was a major part of a more complex system. In addition to your route paralleling the coast, it provided several ways to move goods from the English Channel to the Bay of Biscay. Entering France south of the Channel Islands at St. Malo, traffic moved south to the canalized River Vilaine and to Redon. Redon became an immensely prosperous four-way nautical crossroads that provided south-moving barges three options: straight ahead for the coast at Billiers, right for Pontivy and Brest, or left for Nantes at the mouth of France's greatest river, the Loire.

Alone but Not Lonely

You will be riding 128 miles from Pontivy to Nantes, through the beautifully pastoral countryside of central Brittany. You will pass 106 locks, lovely medieval market towns, forests of oak and pine, and quiet glades of solitude. Between interesting old towns and villages like Josselin, Malestroit, la Gacilly, Redon, and Sucé-sur-Erdre, you may find yourself completely alone for long stretches with only the herons and an occasional swan to keep you company. Lonesome? Need human company, shelter, or supplies? Just follow an intersecting country road or hiking trail toward a town or village. Then return to the waterway when you are surfeited and seek peace once again.

The canal has two summits. The first one is encountered only 4 miles from Pontivy, providing an almost indiscernible downhill trend the rest of the way to Redon. There is a climb to another summit between Blain and Nort-sur-Erdre. From there it is downhill all the way to the sea. No towpath remains along the River Erdre, so for the last 20 miles before Nantes it's necessary to use secondary roads, most of which follow the Erdre, one of France's most beautiful river valleys.

Chapter 14

Backcountry Brittany Along the Canal

From Pontivy to Redon

Pontivy, in the strategic center of Brittany, is a most interesting starting point. It had the good fortune to have as its sponsor Napoleon Bonaparte, at the height of his power. His efforts brought the canal, the canalization of the river Blavet, a new town hall, military barracks, and prosperity. For years the town was called Napoléanville. Pontivy today is a wonderful mixture of Bretagne medieval, Napoleonic, and contemporary French provincial culture.

The Château des Rohan dominates this market town, as it has for more than five centuries. Its stark 64-foot walls, flanked by two towers, were built by Jean II of Rohan, a family name associated for centuries with Breton politics.

Take time to explore the old section of town and search out the Place du Martray, a square bordered by old houses. The sixteenth century Church of Our Lady of Joy is also worth a stop.

Eager to get started? No problem; waterways are everywhere in the center of this interesting old town. Find the one that heads northeast and pedal along the wonderfully smooth and tree-lined path on the right-hand side through a park with benches and picnic tables shaded by huge old trees.

Your introduction to canal cycling starts with a highly unusual segment: one of the densest successions of locks on the entire French waterways system. Within the first 10 miles there are 53 locks. It's a major problem for yachtsmen, but for you, just a gentle incline to the summit. After that it's downhill for the next 62 miles, but you'll scarcely notice it.

An excellent surface continues from Pontivy through a forest glade. Here the path parallels the first of three lock staircases, where locks appear joined at the hip. The path surface becomes potholed after you pass under a railroad bridge. On your right is a large factory.

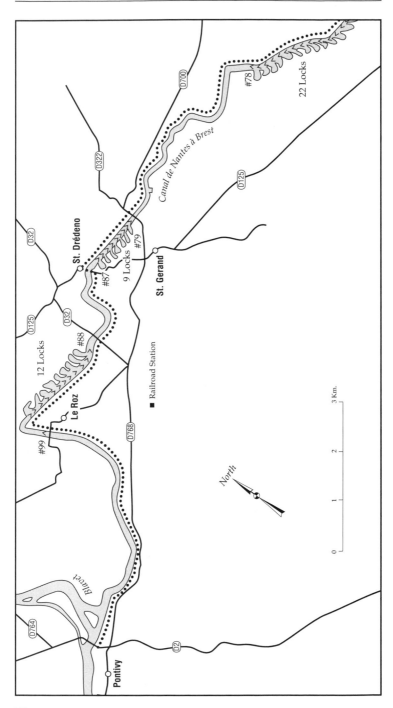

At the Lock le Coudic (No. 87) cross the canal and use the left bank. You should stay on the left side past the two remaining staircases. At the second lock after the final staircase, Coët-prat (No. 55) use the bridge to cross back to the right-hand path and head on toward the crossroads village of Rohan.

At Rohan cross back to the left bank and continue until Lock Griffet (No. 45). Return again to the right bank. At a hamlet called Bocneuf, use the highway bridge for route D 764 to get back on the left side. This is the bridge immediately after Lock Pommeleuc (No. 40). The left side will be your pathway through the major market town of Josselin and all the way to Roc St. André.

A short distance south of Rohan on the left of the canal lies the Abbey de Timadeuc, built in the Cistercian style in 1841 by Trappist monks, who continue in residence. At Lock Timadeuc (No. 50), take D 2 northeast a few hundred yards to visit it.

A mile north of the canal, at Lock Griffet (No. 45), on D 117, in the center of Les Forges sits a *château* in front of which are the well-preserved ruins of a large furnace, built in 1756 by the Rohan family to make cannon from local iron ore and charcoal.

Josselin's medieval charms ought to entice you at least into a lunch stop. If you stay longer there are excellent hotels in the city center, where your window may look out on a scene little changed from the fifteenth century. The town is ranged on a steep hillside overlooking the valley of the canalized River Oust. It is dominated by another huge Rohan family castle, which offers two highly different faces: Facing the river, it is a heavy, unadorned military fortification, while the side facing the town is intricate with decoration, pinnacles, and gardens. The town with its slate roofs rises behind the castle and clusters around the basilica of Our Lady of the Rosebush.

Josselin and its neighbor and rival, Ploermel, provide an interesting historical footnote on how to avoid war. During the fourteenth century, Josselin and the Rohans were backing the royal house of France. The Montforts, headquartered at nearby Ploermel, supported the other side. There had been a number of bloody encounters, then somebody had an idea. Instead of a major battle, why not have each side contribute its 30 best men and let them settle it with pikes, swords, and battle axes. The home team prayed that night in the basilica and they met the next day. Prayers worked. Josselin won and a bloody war was averted. The Battle of 30 is commemorated by a stone pyramid that marks the spot today.

The Josselin basilica dates from the eleventh century and is a good example of flamboyant Gothic. The name goes back to the seventh century, when a peasant is said to have found a statue of the Virgin in a thicket of brambles. When he tried to return it to the brambles, it wouldn't stay, so a church was built to give it sanctuary.

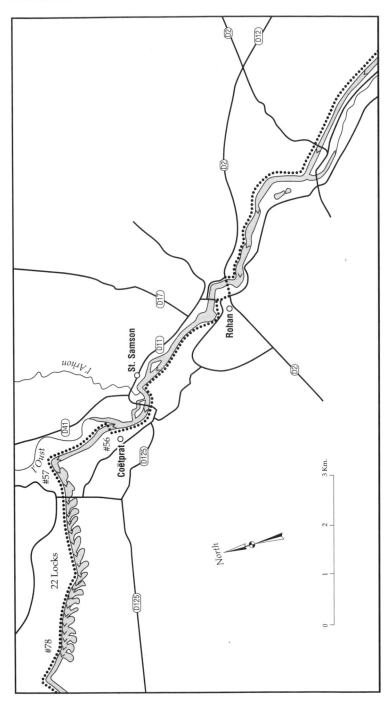

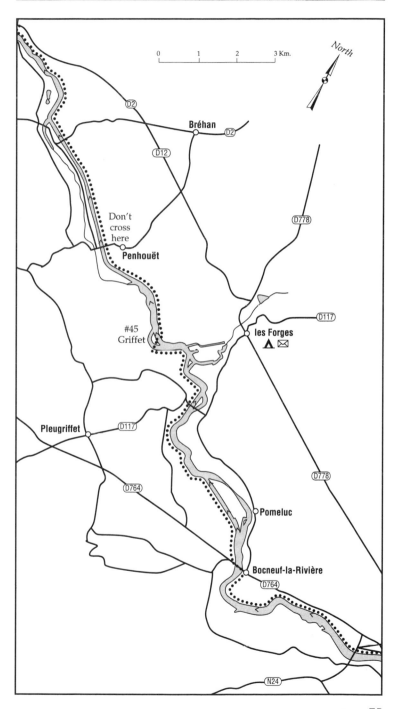

Ploermel, 8 miles away and a little off to the north of your track, was once a seat of the Dukes of Brittany and is also interesting for its church and old homes. You may encounter a statue to a famous son, Dr. Guerin, credited with inventing surgical dressings. The church venerates the town founder, who lived in the sixth century. Noteworthy is the church's whimsically carved door.

Back on the canal, on the left-hand path riding conditions are excellent. At Roc St. André use the bridge for D 4 to get to the right-hand side.

Malestroit is another gem that gleams through its well-preserved antiquity. There are many fifteenth and sixteenth century houses, many with exquisitely carved front doors. The old bridges over the canal and river are interesting as well as the Church of St. Giles, half Romanesque, half Gothic.

The Malestroit *Syndicat*, or tourist office, is located close to the canal on the far side of town, and in its front yard can be seen the homemade sailboat on which an optimistic native of Malestroit managed to sail single-handed across the Atlantic several years ago.

About 2 miles west of town on D 321 is what remains of St. Marcel. On June 18, 1944, the retreating Germans burned it to the ground.

Southeast of Malestroit the excellent surface continues (on the right), a well-used and hard-packed roadway of gravel only occasionally degraded by recent flooding. At the outskirts of Malestroit you will pass the major industry of the region, a large cheese factory.

The village of St. Laurent boasts a small hotel/bar and a picnic area on the canal.

St. Congard is a pleasant little crossroads village with a small municipal campground along the pathway. Cafes and restaurants are handy. It claims as a native son, Nominöe, the first ruler of Brittany. Further on, St. Grave, a short distance off the towpath to the right, has a grocery, post office, a small hotel, *chambres d'hôte,* and a couple of *cafés*.

The canal follows the valley of the River Oust through soft, undulating countryside. In several places the river and canal combine. There are no population centers until the waterway is crossed by highway D 138. For Peillac take a right for about 4 miles. A left for about the same distance will get you to the interesting artisanal village of la Gacilly. Even closer, within a few hundred yards of the canal along D 138 toward Peillac, you will encounter a campground, swimming pool, and several restaurants catering to boaters, campers, and hikers.

Beyond this the canal and river join and rejoin their waters in an intricate series of lagoons and marshes until, after a long straight

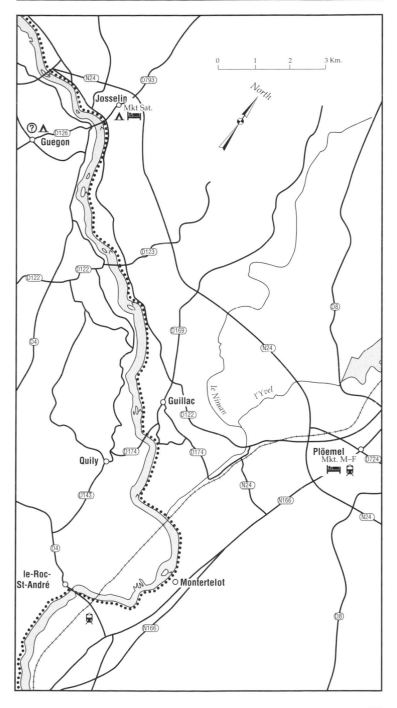

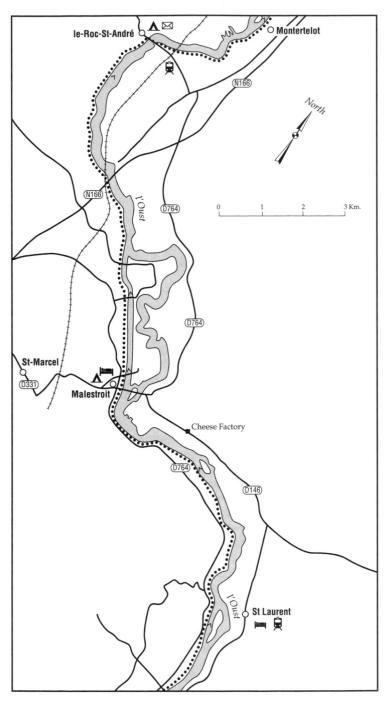

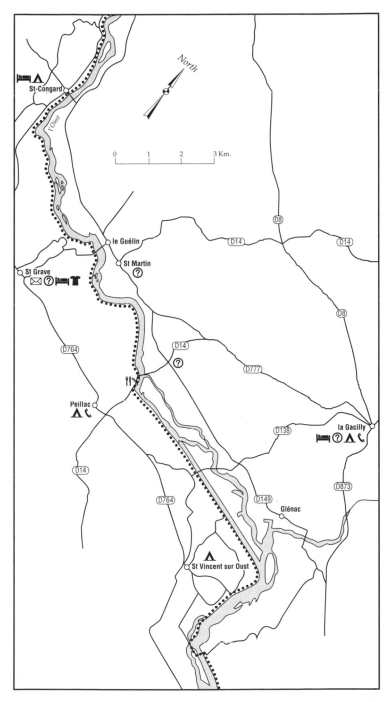

stretch, you arrive at Lock Maclais (No. 19). It is here that a tributary, the Aff, comes in from the north. For a short, but interesting, stretch the waters of the Aff, the Oust, and the canal come together to flow through a narrow gorge. Look carefully at the steep cliff face on the opposite side. You may see mountaineers practicing their climbing skills. A pleasant little picnic ground beside the path with the Celtic name, Ti-Kendal'ch, is a good place for a refreshment break. A sign indicates you are a guest of the commune of St. Vincent-sur-Oust, out of sight above you on the bluff.

In season you might want to rent a canoe here for exploring the Isle aux Pies, which has nothing to do with desserts, but a lot to do with birds, particularly magpies and water fowl. It is a wild marshy area favored by nature lovers and bird watchers, and reaches all the way back to la Gacilly, an unspoiled mini-wilderness. Eel fishing is excellent in these marshes.

As you continue, still on the right side, watch on the opposite bank for a lovely little chapel in a soft, green meadow nearly hidden by trees. Next you will come to Grand Vannage, a sluice gate through which most of the waters of the combined Aff and Oust pass. Use the gate to pass over this stream, then use the picturesque bridge a few yards farther on to cross over to the left bank for the rest of the ride to Redon.

Need a croissant or a cool drink? Follow the little country road to the right immediately after crossing the bridge. In the next tiny hamlet turn left and go up the hill, where you will find a small country store with a good stock of fresh baked goods.

Back on the canal (left bank) the towpath becomes rough from time to time, evidence of winter flooding. As you pass by a major refuse dump, mostly hidden from view, you reflect on the wonderful absence of litter along the routes you are traveling. Litter is almost never seen in France, even in ditches along busy highways.

Where D 764 crosses, there is a traffic circle close to the canal with a typical country inn sited conveniently. Redon's pleasant outskirts start here and within a few hundred yards down a pleasant, smooth lane under the shade of huge trees, you enter the major town of Redon, where you'll find most conveniences including a good bike repair shop and an automatic laundry within a few yards of each other and of the track.

Redon is a good place for major detours north to the channel coast for St. Malo and Mont St. Michel or south toward the Atlantic coast and the Golfe de Morbihan and the important prehistoric remains at Carnac. The train station is located up the hill to your left from the center of town. Can't take the time? Consider following Grande Randonnée GR 39 north from Redon to St. Just. It's only about 10 miles, but the megalithic remains there are second only to Carnac in importance.

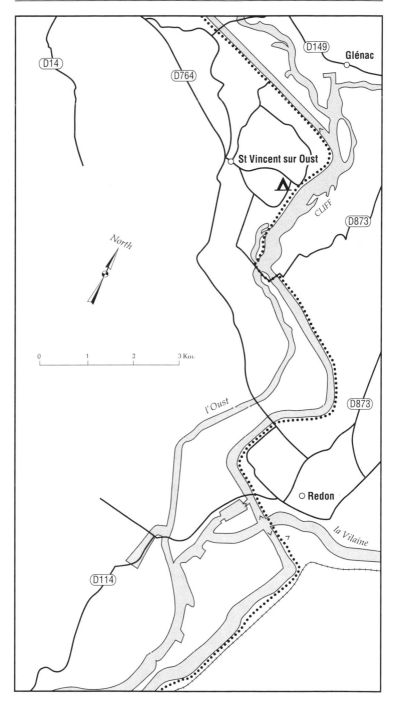

Redon is worthy of a stopover. It is the market for the region and capital of the district of Pays de Vilaine. Check out the four-way canal-river intersection close to the city center and the revitalized city harbor, which at one time was full of salt barges. Today it is full of pleasure boats. Visit the old parts of town, particularly the Grande Rue, with its cobbled streets and overhanging old houses. Saint Saviour's Church is an important specimen of Romanesque style. Its twelfth century free-standing tower is the only one of its kind in Brittany.

From Redon to Glanet

The canal intersection with the fast-flowing River Vilaine must pose a small problem for canal boats trying to cross it, particularly during springtime high water, when the river fights hard to keep the boats from re-entering the sylvan waters of the canal. Cyclists have no problem. They just take the highway bridge over the river and head off toward Nantes, following the left-hand path.

Look back over your left shoulder for a glimpse of the eleventh century tower of Saint Saviour, which dominates the town. Behind you on the opposite side are ancient salt warehouses, vital to the trade that made Redon an important inland port.

You leave town on a fine, hard-surfaced road, which passes close to a large *supermarché*. It may be a good time to stock up. Market towns will be scarce for the next few days. Within sight of Redon, the canal takes a 90-degree turn to head due south. You are in the suburb of St. Nicholas de Redon. On your left is a *gendarmarie* post. The country here is very flat, so the battlements of Redon stay in view for a while behind you. The path continues to be a minor highway for several miles and runs along between a railroad close on the left and the canal on the right. Beyond the third bridge, the road changes from asphalt to smooth gravel and moves through a cut.

On the opposite side of the canal is an old boat graveyard. Long-abandoned wooden hulls lying in the woods, and partially submerged along the bank breed unanswered questions.

About 7 miles from Redon, a canal comes in from the right, forming a water link with the River Vilaine. Just south of the junction, cross the bridge and proceed down the right side of the canal, a smooth, hard surface. On the right, on the riverbank, is a small marina with camping facilities. The combination canal path/country road bears slightly to the right of the canal and a line of ubiquitous poplar trees separates you from the canal for a time. Further to the right is the large, open, and seemingly empty expanse of the river valley.

After a short detour away from the canal, the road/path returns. Take the bridge back to the left bank and follow a good

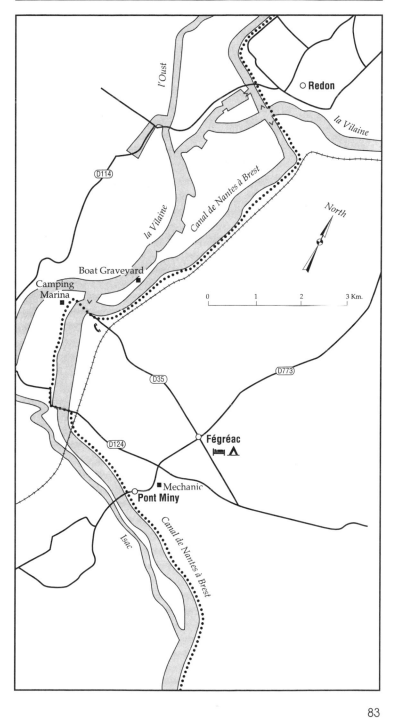

gravel pathway. Within a few hundred yards, the railroad cross-es the canal and it may be necessary to dismount to pass under the bridge. The pathway deteriorates after a little while, due to serious flooding during the winter of 1995.

Things improve at the village of Fégréac, where there is a nice park on the right bank. On the left is La Maison du Canal, which offers regional information, modern toilets, and overnight accommodations. From here follow the left bank on a fine, well-maintained gravel path.

Evidence of heavy flooding continues for about 5 miles to Guenrouet. Here nothing disturbs the tranquillity of the wet world except an occasional heron or a water animal jumping for safety as your wheels bear down on him.

At a wide swing of the canal you arrive at the port of St. Clair. On the right-hand bank is a small marina for pleasure boaters, several attractive restaurants, and a large campground. To get to them and to the village of Guenrouet, up on the bluff, cross on the bridge and follow D 2 up the steep hill. Here you'll find a *crêperie, tabacs, cafés,* a *charcuterie, épicerie,* and a small hotel.

If you need a train to get back to civilization, continue on D 2 to St. Gildas des Bois, about 7 miles.

Ride back down the hill to the canal, cross the bridge to the left bank, and rejoin the path under the shadow of a heroic cross with altar, which acts in summer as an open-air sanctuary for campers. The canal path is smooth gravel, and its curves conform exactly to the curves of the canal, which in this sector has a strong current and acts much more like a river than a canal. Just beyond the first long curve, the path passes beneath a sharp, wooded bluff on which are sited a number of impressive homes. The most impressive is the Domaine de Carheil, a magnificent old manor.

Along this section of the canal path you will often encounter barricades with signs saying: "*Interdit sauf Authorisation.*" Not to worry, the signs are addressing motor vehicles, not cyclists. Sometimes the barricades are down, but no matter, there will be a well-worn track around them. The canal here traverses a dense forest. Soon you will come to a pretty, little hand-operated lock, Ecluse Melneuf (No. 16).

The towpath continues as well-maintained gravel and is a real pleasure to ride. Here, the military row of poplars has been replaced by another military cordon, this time plane trees, which keep solid company with your left elbow. A few hundred yards beyond the D 3 bridge, you will come upon another lock, Touche (No. 15). This one is in the middle of rushing water, which gushes noisily over a weir on the far side.

Within a half mile you will come to a major highway bridge, which carries Route D 81 directly southeast to Nantes. Moving on

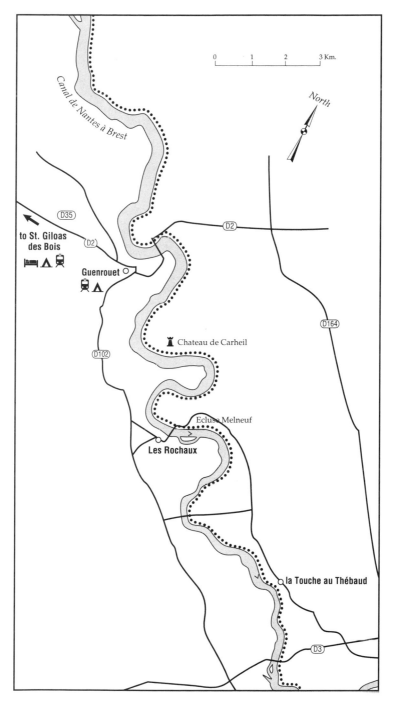

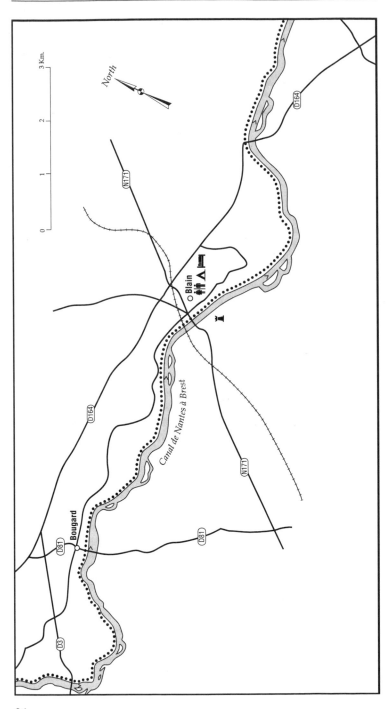

Author's Note

Some of the research for this section of my book took place in March 1995, only a couple of months after major flooding. No one had bothered to post a warning for cyclists. Suddenly I found that the small puddle I was in seemed to have no end. And the water got deeper, sometimes to the sprockets. Soon there was only a border of tall grass on my right and the border of ever-present trees to my left to confirm I was still on the path.

To give up while still relatively dry, turn around, getting soaked in the process, and head back to dry land—or continue on? A major decision. I pressed on. Only the bottoms of my packs and my shoes and socks were wet when I finally emerged from the flood, as I had managed somehow to stay upright. Next time I'll consider packing a lifeboat.

through alternately wooded and pastoral countryside without much sign of humanity, there is only one more lock, La Paudais (No. 12), to pass before you approach a population center, Blain. You will pass under a railroad bridge, then the bridge carrying heavily traveled N 171, which links the coast at St. Nazaire with Châteaubriant.

A detour for supplies or accommodations to Blain can be made just ahead of the N 171 highway bridge. Turn left to a small traffic circle and follow the signs up the hill to the town, where you'll find most all amenities. Also a camping location is just off the canal's right bank not far from the highway bridge. On the left bank is an attractive new port for the accommodation of pleasure boats. The complex, facing the canal and a lovely turreted castle beyond, includes several inns and restaurants with modern restrooms.

The towpath on from Blain is hard-surfaced and continues on the left bank for a mile or so before it alternates between paved surface and gravel until you get to the next lock. The next bridge, D 37, is at la Chevallerais, a combination bird sanctuary and forest park with an elaborate sign welcoming visitors and detailing the charms of the region. There are picnic tables and barbecues amid most pleasant surroundings.

Just beyond the little park at la Chevallerais you will encounter another lock, after which the path deteriorates, becoming rampant with potholes. Fortunately the bad section lasts less than a mile. When you come to the bridge carrying N 137 you are at the canal summit, the highest point between Pontivy and Nantes. Another small park commemorates canal construction and elaborate displays inform passersby that construction of the reservoirs that supply the canal was started under Napoleon I in 1812, using

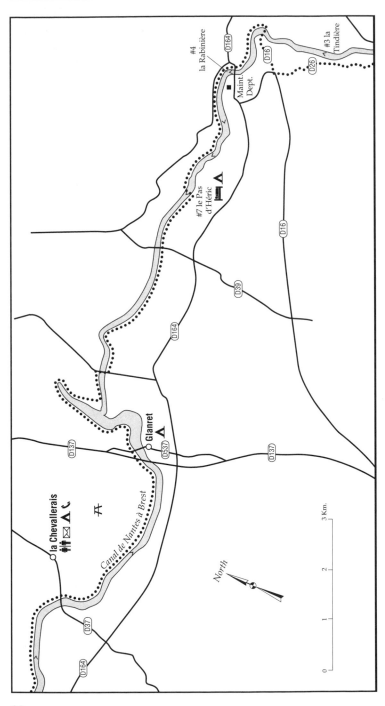

Spanish war prisoners as principal labor. However, work was suspended two years later, when the Spaniards rebelled against the harsh conditions. Work was resumed in 1822 without slaves.

If your day is ending here, you're in luck. Just continue on to the bridge carrying N 137, at a hamlet called Glanet. Hang a right over the canal and follow the signs taking you on the original highway, generally parallel to the modern highway, toward an inn called l'Abreuvoir, run by Thierry Amirault. The inn is a tastefully restored *manoir* where the welcome is hearty, the fire on the hearth bright, and you can get a memorable meal, with Beethoven playing softly in the background.

From Glanet to Nantes

From Glanet the path continues to hug the left bank of the canal as it nears its eastern terminus at the tidal river Erdre. On the left is a substantial reservoir, which supplies water to the canal. The path ends after following a canal arm. No problem, just follow the only option you have, a path that goes off sharply to the left, then continue making turns to the right on a series of small farm roads to bring you back to the canal bank.

At the next bridge, cross the canal and follow the right bank on a well-graded, packed sand and gravel surface. Pass under an elevated pipeline that crosses the canal. Here the path is high above the canal level, obviously not the original hauling track. When you come to the first lock, Pas d'Héric (No. 7), it's necessary to cross on the lock to resume travel on the left-hand path.

Here the canal makes a number of sharp bends. It meanders under several ancient bridges, and you ride in pleasant solitude past a series of locks that come up in quick succession. Ironically, the path deteriorates to a couple of ruts in the grass just beyond a canal maintenance yard, but take heart, the end is near.

To continue to Nantes, it's necessary to abandon the deteriorating towpath and the terminating canal right here and take to the highways. (Towpaths do not currently exist along most French rivers.) Leave the peace and security of the canal path at the second bridge after Lock la Rabinière (No. 4). This is D 16, a heavily traveled truck route, but you need stay with it for only a mile. Take a left at D 26 and head through high pastoral farm country toward the hamlet of Casson. There is a pair of interesting old towers as you enter the village. You are heading toward one of the most beautiful valleys of France, as you take D 37 out of Casson toward Sucé-sur-Erdre.

You glide past an impressive old folks home as you get a nice, long coast into Sucé. To your left in the center of town is a modern marina. You should now be following D 69, and the signs point you toward la Chapelle-sur-Erdre and Nantes. The

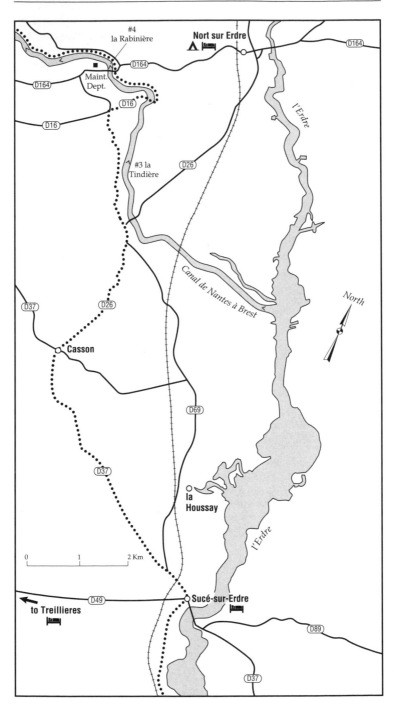

Nort sur Erdre

#4
la Rabinière

D164

Maint.
Dept.

D164

D164

D16

D16

#3 la
Tindière

D26

l'Erdre

Canal de Nantes à Brest

D37

D26

North

Casson

D69

D37

la
Houssay

l'Erdre

0   1   2 Km

D49

Sucé-sur-Erdre

to Treillieres

D89

D37

highway gets busier as you close with the city, but it has reasonable shoulders. The foul air blasts of passing 18-wheelers helps you appreciate canal paths. At la Chapelle follow the signs: *toutes directions*, around five traffic circles before you leave the town.

At the Nantes city line, D 69 passes over a superhighway and takes you around still another traffic circle, off of which you can take a green-marked bicycle route. This gets you to one of the city's main shopping streets, Boulevard Robert Schumann. If you stay with it, you will pass through the city's center and quickly arrive at Nantes' impressive rail station and the Loire River. Close by you'll find the tourist office.

Nantes is a bustling river and ocean port, a city of more than a quarter million people. It is not strictly Breton, but rather is the capital of the Pays de Loire. It was first Celtic, then Roman, and in the seventh century was ravaged by the Normans, who came by sea and spread over Brittany. They were finally driven out by a Breton expatriate, Alain Barbe-Torte, who returned a conquering hero from exile in England.

From the sixteenth to the eighteenth century, Nantes grew rich on the "ebony trade," a euphemism for the circular commerce that took slaves from Africa to the West Indies and sugar from there to Brittany where it was refined and shipped inland up the Loire. It was good business for Nantes entrepreneurs who made as much as 200 percent profit on each trip. Their prosperity is evidenced by the homes they built along the Quay de la Fosse.

The French Revolution killed the slave trade. The sugar trade was far less profitable, and new ships with deeper draft found the Loire too shallow. For a period Nantes fell upon hard times. But in the twentieth century, new dredging methods once again made the harbor viable and the Nantais turned to diversified industry for their future. Today the city prospers once again.

Not far from the station are the massive and somber walls of the Ducal Castle, built by François II in 1466. It was here in 1578 that Henry IV signed the Edict of Nantes, granting limited freedom of religion. Today the castle houses a number of interesting museums. Opposite the castle is the Cathedral of Saint Peter and Saint Paul, which was begun in the thirteenth century. It has a magnificent carved doorway, two square towers, and interior vaulting higher than that of either Notre Dame or Westminster Abbey.

You might want to check out the *Passage Pommerage*, a shopping arcade full of elegant stores dating from the middle of the last century. Other visits to consider: Fine Arts Museum, Nantes Zoo, Botanical Gardens, Natural History Museum or the Palais Dobrée, a nineteenth century mansion, and next door, the former country house of the bishops of Nantes.

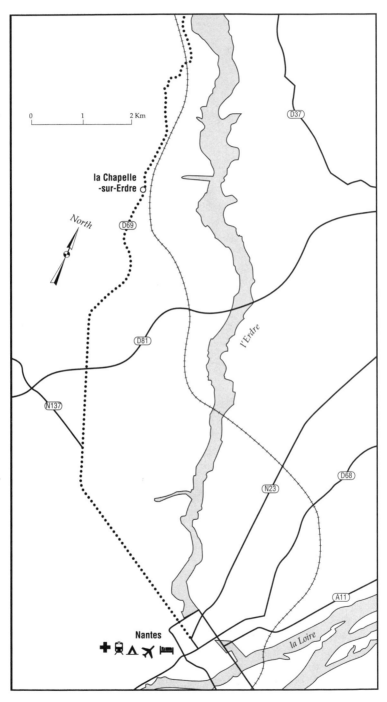

Chapter 15

Canal Nantes à Brest— Accommodations

Hotels, Guest Houses, Campgrounds, Phone Numbers, and Other Useful Information

Note: Communities are listed in order geographically from Pontivy toward the river/seaport of Nantes. Numbers following hotel and guest house listings indicate number of rooms; those following campground listings indicate number of campsites. Number following community name is ZIP code. Stars are the government luxury rating.

Pontivy 56300 (Market: Monday)

Hotels		
la Terrasse*	15	97 25 51 11
l'Europe**	20	97 25 11 14
Robic**	25	97 25 11 80
Martin**	23	97 25 11 80
le Porhoët**	28	97 25 34 88
le Rohan-Wesserling***	27	97 25 02 01
le Napoléon*	13	97 25 13 58
la Villeneuve**	10	97 39 83 10
Youth Hostel		
Auberge de Jeunesse	13	97 25 58 27
Camping		
du Doric**		97 27 92 20
Hospital		
Tourist Office		97 25 04 10

Rohan 56580

Hotel		
de Rohan		57 51 50 61
Camping		
Municipal		57 51 50 33
Tourist Office		97 51 30 33

Les Forges 56120

Camping
Cadoret**   200   97 75 31 27

Guiegon 56120

Hotel
les Quatre Vents   5   97 22 21 68
Guest House
le Val aux Houx   97 22 24 32
Camping
du Bas de la Lande   70   97 22 22 20

Josselin 56120 (Market: Saturday)

Hotels
Relais de l'Oust**   25   97 75 63 06
du Château**   36   97 22 20 11
de France**   21   97 22 23 06
l'Escale   5   97 22 39 31
le Pelican   7   97 22 22 05
Guest Houses
Alain Bignon   97 22 22 62
M. Guyot   97 22 22 09
Mme Josephe Le Goff   97 22 37 44
M. Robic   97 22 31 44
M. Robinson   97 22 29 97
Camping
de Guiegon   97 22 22 20
Hospital   97 73 13 13
Tourist Office   97 22 36 43

Ploermel 56800 (Market: Monday and Friday morning)

Hotels
la Boule d'Or   12   97 74 05 21
le Cobh***   13   97 74 00 49
le Roi Arthur***   46   97 73 64 64
les Arcades   8   97 74 01 05
le Commerce**   19   97 74 05 32
St. Marc**   9   97 74 00 01
les Routiers   10   97 74 00 48
Hospital   97 74 21 11
Tourist Office   97 74 02 70

Roc St. André 56460

Camping
Municipal**   50   97 74 93 53

Malestroit 56140 (Market: Thursday morning)
Hotels
St. Michel	8	97 75 13 01
Manoir de la Combe	10	97 26 90 65
Le Canotier		97 75 08 69

Guest Houses
la Garmanière	97 75 20 27
Mmc Reynard	97 75 12 09
Mme Lanoe	97 75 05 39

Camping
La Daufresne**	100	97 75 13 33
Hospital		97 75 20 46
Tourist Office		97 75 14 57

St. Congard 56140
Camping
Municipal	97 43 50 13

St. Martin-sur-Oust 56200
Hotels
du Guelin	14	99 91 55 90
Château de Castellan	5	99 91 51 69

Guest House
le Bois de Haut	2	99 91 55 57

Camping
la Digue	99 91 55 76

Peillac 56220
Hotel
Chez Antoine**	99 91 24 43

Camping
le Pont d'Oust	99 91 36 01
Tourist Office	99 91 36 01

St. Grave 56220
Hotel
Le Lon d'Or	97 43 54 70

Guest House
M. Clodic	97 43 54 71

Camping
la Grange aux Moines	5	97 43 54 71

Glenac 56200

Guest House		
Mme Soudy, Colomel		99 71 20 86
Camping		
le Bourg**		99 08 13 62
Ile aux Pies**		99 91 71 41

La Gacilly 56200

Hotels		
de France**	40	99 08 11 15
Chandouineau**		99 71 02 04
du Square**	38	99 08 11 15
Camping		
la Gacilly***		99 08 15 28
Tourist Office		99 08 21 75

Carentoir 56200

Hotel		
Club Pre Gallo	18	99 08 84 85

St. Vincent-sur-Oust 56200

Camping		
de Painfaut**		99 91 24 34

Redon 44460 (Market: Monday)

Hotels		
le France**	20	99 71 06 11
Asthir Hotel**	18	99 71 10 91
Chandouineau**	7	99 71 02 04
la Belle Anguille	5	99 72 31 02
Auberge des Marais	6	99 71 02 48
Marmotte*	38	99 72 71 71
le Gaudence**	18	99 71 91 12
Camping		
la Goule d'Eau**		99 72 14 39
le Lot à Rieux		99 91 90 25
le Morinais		99 72 12 17
Youth Hostel		
Auberge de Jeunesse		99 72 14 39
Hospital		99 71 71 71
Tourist Office		99 71 06 04

St. Nicholas de Redon 44460

Hotels		
Bel Hotel**	34	99 71 10 10
Bonotel**	32	99 72 23 23

Fégréac 44460
Guest House		
Coisnaute	3	40 91 27 19
Camping		
le Bellion**	15	40 91 20 21
Maison de Canal	9	40 91 24 96

Guenrouet 44530
Camping		
St. Clair**	120	40 87 61 52
Halte Nautique	6	40 87 68 09

St. Gildas des Bois 44530
Guest House		
la Ferme Ecole	2	40 66 90 27
Camping		
de Bournegat	10	40 01 42 29

Blain 44130
Hotels		
la Gerbc de Blé**	10	40 79 10 50
le Grand Cerf*	9	40 79 00 47
le Port*	10	40 79 01 22
Guest Houses		
la Mercerais	2	40 79 04 30
la Gravier		40 79 10 25
Camping		
le Château**	45	40 79 11 00
Tourist Office		40 87 15 11

Héric 44810
Hotel		
l'Abreuvoir**	9	40 57 63 81
Camping		
la Pindière**	33	40 57 65 41

Nort-sur-Erdre 44390
Hotels		
le Bretagne**	42	40 66 55 66
le Commerce	7	40 72 20 53
les Trois Marchands		40 72 20 34
Camping		
Port Mulon**		40 72 23 57
du Foue Bodebril		40 79 19 91

Sucé-sur-Erdre 44240
Hotel
au Cordon Bleu   8   40 77 71 34
Tourist Office   40 77 70 66

Treillières 44119
Hotel
Relais Mercure Nantes Nord   40 72 87 88

Nantes 44000
Nantes is one of the country's major cities, a flourishing river and seaport with a magnificent heritage. It is a lively city, proud of its municipal gardens and parks and full of archaeological monuments celebrating its rich past. Modern rail and air service provide easy access to the rest of the country and the world. Scores of hotels of every class are available. For a complete list, contact the Tourist Office, 40 47 04 51 (fax 40 89 11 99).
Youth Hostel
la Manu   70   40 20 57 25
Camping
le Val du Cens****   200   40 74 47 94
Hospital
Emergency Medical   40 08 37 77

Chapter 16

About the Region—
The Garonne Valley,
Gascony, and the Midi

How to Get There and Back
Agen, the start of the Midi tour, is best reached by train from
Paris (Gare Montparnasse). Excellent service links Paris and
Bordeaux via ultra-fast TGV trains. Often a change of trains is
mandated in Bordeaux for Agen. Total time: about five hours. To
return to Paris after concluding your ride to the sea, at Narbonne
take a train that parallels your bike route back to Toulouse and
Bordeaux and on to the capital.

About Your Route
Cyclists who have experienced Brittany and Burgundy via
the water roads will notice a major difference when they saddle
up at Agen and head toward the blue Mediterranean Sea, nearly 260 miles away.

Along this historic route you will seldom be alone. The
route you will be following, first the Canal Lateral à la Garonne
and then at Toulouse the Canal du Midi, are simply the remnants of an earlier transport system, succeeded in modern times
by a major rail line, and even more recently by an important segment of France's new ultra-modern highway network. The
high-speed rail line and the superhighway will drift back and
forth over your head for the duration of your seaward ride. Also
keeping company will be an even earlier transport artery, the
rivers Garonne, Tarn, and a number of lesser ones, all of which
gave birth to the canal idea hundreds of years ago.

The presence of the trains and the hurrying motorists won't
cause you any grief at all. But you will feel a quickened pulse
that is missing in Brittany and Burgundy.

Your path from Agen curves gently in a southeasterly direction, then due east to meet the sea about 40 miles from the Spanish border. In the process it takes you through rich agricultural

valleys, the center of Toulouse, France's aerospace capital, and among picturesque towns and villages where history goes back before the Romans to the Phoenicians and the Greeks.

There are probably more vineyards along your route than in any other part of France, as the Canal du Midi murmurs past the

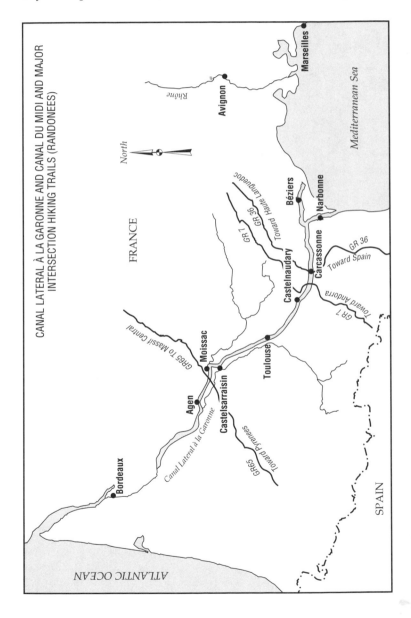

rich wine regions of Corbières on your right and Minervois on your left.

The perpetually snow-capped Pyrenees marking the Spanish border also accompany you from Toulouse onward, a scant 50 miles to the south.

At the outskirts of Toulouse, the River Garonne diverges and heads toward its source in the high Pyrenees, and your canal becomes the Canal du Midi, one of the oldest in Europe. Negotiating the modern streets of Toulouse poses no major problem to the cyclist, and soon you find yourself on the far side of the city experiencing a superhighway made just for cyclists.

Your route to the sea passes through ancient fortified villages, past Romanesque and medieval abbeys and churches and eventually under the very ramparts of Carcassonne, perhaps the best-preserved, most photographed, and most extensive medieval relic in all of Europe. Pleasant villages like Moissac, Montauban, and Castelnaudary wait peacefully to welcome you.

Because the pleasure boat business along the Midi has grown exponentially in recent years, facilities for travelers, both waterborne and cycling, have grown too. Many villages have added small marinas equipped with restaurants, shower rooms, and camping areas to persuade travelers to stop. But even without the new canalside facilities, the frequency of hotels and good restaurants in this region far surpasses that of Brittany or Burgundy.

From Toulouse you will have a little more than 100 miles of easy cycling along this old canal. At first there is a scarcely noticeable uphill grade to the summit at Narouze, about 30 miles away. From there it is all downhill to a canal junction just west of Narbonne, where you take a right to the city and beyond a few more miles, to your first sight of the sea among the sand dunes.

A Bit of History

The ancient name for the region is Languedoc, which once covered all of southern France, and at the time divided the nation linguistically. Languedoc means the language of Oc (Occitan) as distinguished from the northerners, who spoke French. Today a losing battle is being fought by local linguists to hold to their old language and customs. If you are lucky you may encounter a festival, one of many designed to honor and preserve the old language and culture.

Languedoc has a long and bloody history, and many battles of the Albigension Crusade were fought here. It was a particularly ugly religious war, which annihilated an early Christian heretic sect, the Cathars. Their extreme teachings had migrated to southern France from Bulgaria in the tenth century. The Cathars were adherents of the pure life who denied the basic

Christian beliefs of incarnation, virgin birth, the Trinity, and God's omnipotence. Their extreme asceticism included the rejection of all material things, marriage, violence, and even the bearing of children.

Amazingly, they flourished, but that did not make them popular with the papacy. The popes put pressure on them, which climaxed with the crusade in 1211. Simon de Montfort led an army representing the papacy and a number of battles took place at various points along your route, eventually spelling *fini* to the Cathars.

As in most parts of France and Europe, wars seem to have taken up more time than peace. The Hundred Years War against England was one of these, with lesser wars also leaving their scars.

Churches

Many devotees of ancient architecture collect Romanesque churches the way others collect stamps or coins. For them, the towns and villages along the Midi provide a rich lore. These early churches, predating the Gothic era by 400 to 500 years, dot the countryside, and many are used still. They are characterized by their lower silhouette and an austerity and simplicity of line that approaches earthiness.

The cloister within the Abbaye St. Pierre at Moissac is considered the largest and most perfect example of Romanesque church architecture in France. "But," writes Robert Payne in *The Splendor of France*, "it is the gateway [to the cathedral] which one remembers most, and sometimes I think that if everything in France had to be destroyed and one object was allowed to remain, I would choose that gateway."

Cities and Towns

Population centers are larger and more dense along this route than either of the other two routes covered. Agen, Toulouse, Carcassonne, and Narbonne are all busy commercial cities offering virtually every modern amenity. Agen is the capital of the Middle Garonne region and in 1990 was voted the "happiest" city in France.

Toulouse is, of course, France's scientific and technology center, with a bustling university and lots of space-age business to transact. And Narbonne counts its birthdays from 118 B.C., not even counting another three or four centuries before that when the inhabitants just lived there without calling it a city.

In between the busy cities your towpath is flanked by a series of important market towns with comfortable accommodations, good restaurants, and shopping. Don't miss exploring pleasant towns like Valance d'Agen, Moissac, Castelnaudary.

Many of the towns and villages along your route carry the prefix *"castelnau."* It refers to communities that sprang up outside of the walls of a castle.

Another special community is the *bastide*, perhaps the earliest known example of community planning. Organized for mutual convenience as well as defense, many of the bastides required their citizens to sign charters agreeing to a strict set of rights and duties. The idea must have had some merit as some are still flourishing after 900 years. Several excellent examples near your route include: Beaumont-de-Lomagne, Realville, Montjoi, and Castelsagrat.

Food and Drink

If there is one adjective that covers the cuisine of the Midi, it must be "hearty." Characteristic of this peasant heartiness is *cassoulet*, the stew that seems to have its capital in Castelnaudary, but that is available and promoted almost everywhere. Another regional favorite is *cargolade*, also a stew, this one made with snails, lamb, and sausage.

Regional foods are heavily laced with garlic, and lemon marinade is often used. Try leek fritters and when near the coast, octopus. Local cheeses include roquefort and pelardon, a goat cheese.

As your route for many miles is squeezed between two of France's most productive wine-producing regions, the Minervois and Corbières, wine (almost always red, and as hearty as the cuisine) figures prominently at every table. It is generally inexpensive and, in fact, eating out in this region is one of the real bargains of France.

Industry

Except in the Toulouse area, industry in this region is mostly related to agriculture. In the north around Agen and Moissac the principal products are peaches, melons, apples, cherries, kiwis, and strawberries. Moissac is known as the capital of the table grape industry, and its grape variety has its own *appelation controlée* or proprietary label.

In net worth it is the wine that contributes the largest share. Labels such as Fitou, Blanquette de Limoux, Clape, Minervois, Corbières, Quatorze are noteworthy. Tourist offices can provide detailed guides on how to locate each sub-region.

In addition to the Airbus, Concorde, and a wide variety of space vehicles and satellites, Toulouse produces much of France's space-age components.

Chapter 17

Riquet and His Dream

The route you are about to follow to the Mediterranean is the brainchild of one man, a bureaucrat, named Pierre Paul Riquet. At the very outset of the age of canals more than 300 years ago, he conceived the idea of a waterway linking the Atlantic with the Mediterranean, from the head of navigation on the Garonne to the Mediterranean near Narbonne. Almost single-handedly he sold it to the monarchy, directed the extensive excavation, designed the lock system, and invested his own money to save the project from foundering. And when it was completed, his heirs ran it as a business for generations.

All this happened not long after the Mayflower ran aground at Plymouth. At the time it was the most ambitious construction project in the world, with more than 12,000 men involved in the tremendous earth-moving projects. Topographical and water supply problems seemed insurmountable and almost were. Riquet's breakthrough came with the successful completion of the Canal de Briare in 1663, linking the rivers Seine and Loire far to the north. That project, which Riquet studied firsthand, gave him his degree in hydraulics, but even more important, the confidence that his linking the Garonne with the Mediterranean was attainable.

In the same year, taking along the local archbishop for support, Riquet presented his plan and sold it to King Louis XIV's Finance Minister Colbert, who in turn sold it to his boss. A key to the project's practicality and acceptance by Versailles was Riquet's detailed program for water supply. He proposed diverging two major streams from mountains to the north, to the highest point of the canal at Narouze. As a kicker, he told the court he would pay for the water supply problem out of his own pocket. It was a deal the king couldn't pass up.

Riquet delivered the needed water, and in 1666 the king put up money for the canal itself. But even with government backing,

Aqueduct Argentdouble carries the canal and its towpaths high over a tributary of the river Aude south of Laredorte.

from time to time Riquet and his family continued to contribute, a factor that put them into lucrative administrative control for many of the canal's most successful years.

Work was begun on the first lock at Toulouse in 1667 and the section from Toulouse to Trèbes, just beyond Carcassonne, was completed five years later. Riquet's initial design for locks had to be re-drawn and several of the first ones had to be re-placed in favor of a new oval shape, characteristic of some of the Midi locks today.

In 1672 the construction of the final segment, Trèbes to Sète, was started and as anticipated, was the most difficult due to many river crossings. Providing aqueducts to carry the canal over the rivers and thus making them immune to flooding and silting was another of Riquet's contributions to canal science. In all, 55 of them were built.

It was in the final phase of excavation, scarcely 24 miles from the sea, that Riquet's greatest crisis occurred. Progress was halted at Mt. Enserune and it seemed to be an insurmountable barrier. Work stopped abruptly and many felt the entire project would be abandoned. Riquet noted that a small tunnel already existed to divert water under the mountain. Again backing his ideas with action, he concentrated all his workers to prove that the canal could continue by drilling through the mountain. Within a year, the tunnel was completed and the way to the sea stretched level and unobstructed before him.

Riquet, in poor health from his exertions, never saw his dream realized. He died shortly thereafter. Work continued, however, and in 1681 the canal was completed, filled, and opened to traffic.

During most of the succeeding 300 years, Riquet's dream was fully exploited. The canal not only carried most of the imports and exports of the Langueduc region, it also carried passenger boats and was a major national defense artery.

With minor modifications Riquet's original waterway will be your intimate companion for the next 114 miles, very much as Pierre Paul Riquet conceived it more than 300 years ago. The basic locks (114 of them to the sea), the towpath, the aqueducts, the bridges, and the feeder systems are, for the most part, original and intact.

But there have been a few major changes. Many of the locks have been electrified and some have been replaced by a *pente d'eau*, a massive machine that hauls an entire lock—and the boats it contains—up or down a giant inclined plane. You can see this technical marvel just before you get to Montech and the cut-off for Montaubin.

The foremost improvement was the canalization of the River Garonne from Toulouse to the Atlantic at Bordeaux, but that didn't take place until the mid-1800s. Your pathway from Agen to Toulouse will follow this more recent addition to the system.

The greatest threat to the Midi came in this century when commercial barge traffic was displaced by competition from the railroad and trucks. For a time, as with other French canals, competition threatened closure of the entire system. Just in time came the rapid growth of inland cruising, which today is reinvigorating the economy of canalside towns and villages.

Chapter 18

From Agen to Narbonne Along the Canal Lateral à la Garonne

K ick-off place for your ride toward the sea is Agen, the prune capital of France and the principal town of the *département* of Lot-et-Garonne. In 1990 it was voted the most pleasant city in France. It is steeped in history, much of it bloody. For two centuries it was no-man's land between the French and English frontiers, and in the twelfth alone it changed hands 11 times.

The River Garonne was navigable from Bordeaux to Agen before the building of the Canal Lateral à la Garonne in the mid-nineteenth century, and Agen was a busy river port before it became a canal port. The quays and walls of the old port can still be seen. Don't head off without giving Agen a look. One of the major sights is the aqueduct that carries the canal over the River Garonne on the city's western edge. Built in 1843, the immense water bridge has 23 arches. Other places of interest in the city: the eleventh century St. Caprais Cathedral, the Church of the Jacobins, whose interior pillars support a vault built in the shape of a palm tree, renaissance houses of the old town, and the Museum of Fine Art, which is home to the Roman "Venus du Mas" and paintings by Goya, Sisley, Dufy, and others.

Getting off the train in Agen you don't have far to look to find the canal and your start-off point. Take a left out of the train station and climb the iron stairs leading to a pedestrian bridge over the train tracks. The bridge ends at a busy highway. Immediately on the other side is the canal and to the right is a small basin with a marina for rental boats. Saltwater is about 200 miles to the southeast. Unfortunately a few of those miles, of necessity, are on busy highways because at this writing parts of the towpath are nonexistent. Fortunately, the detour is short, and for the most part the ancient towpath is today ideally suited to cycles. In some places it is as close to perfect cycling as is possible.

Just beyond the yacht basin, take the bridge to get over to the towpath on the left side, and stay with it as you move through Agen's residential area. You will pass under a railroad bridge and past another yacht marina as the town peters out. So does the canal path. For the next 7 or 8 miles, until you get to Lock No. 31, La Magistère, the towpath is either marginal or nonexistent. Don't fight it. At the second bridge beyond the yacht marina, take a left on D 443 and detour the nonexistent path. Within a few hundred yards, you will arrive at the heavily traveled N 113, which if you hadn't bought this book, is the route you would be suffering all the next 200 miles. But you know better, so you'll use it only briefly.

You pass through a wide place in the highway called La Fox. Continue on following the signs pointing toward La Magistère and Valance d'Agen. The only thing good about N 113 is the proliferation of highway services. A couple of attractive restaurants here cater to the hurrying traveler. It's recommended that you stay with N 113 for a while longer, particularly if your bike is heavy-laden, as the paralleling towpath is only marginal. At the village of St. Jean de Thurac, if you're hungry for something other than foie gras, check out La Californian, an attractive restaurant on the highway. Link up again with the canal and get away from the uglies of infernal combustion engines when the highway and canal meet near the hamlet of Cavaillé. The path won't win any prizes, but you are back along the canal and you don't have to dodge traffic. Up on a sharp hill to your left oblique, a charming castle looks down on your route, and if you turn 40 degrees to your right, your eyes will flick through four or five centuries, as they sight in on the two huge towers of a modern nuclear power plant. Continue on the left bank of the canal to Les Parieres and use D 30 to cross over to the right bank just short of the turning basin.

Here path conditions improve considerably, but even better is the small country road that parallels the path, one row of lovely trees removed. You rejoin the path at Lock 31, Lamagistère, staying between the medieval castle and the nuclear power plant. Lamagistère was a major stopping point on the canal, and the ruins of its former prominence can still be seen along the path. The towpath is in good condition as it shares an aqueduct and passes over a small river. Here the canal is the center of attention as all transport modes squeeze together in this narrow valley. Close on your right is the ubiquitous highway N 113, then the main line railroad track, then a canal feeding the nuclear plant, and beyond the River Garonne. All are within a few hundred yards of each other.

Soon both the rail and the highway cross your path and take to the other side, and the towpath gets squeezed between the

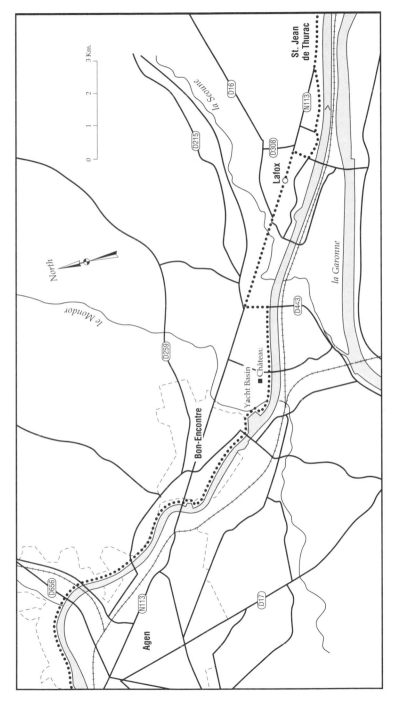

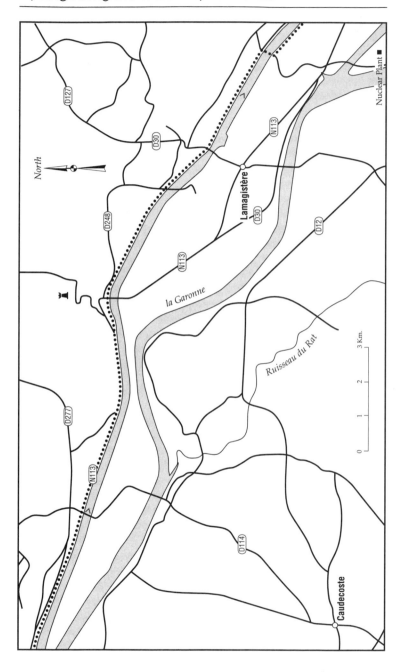

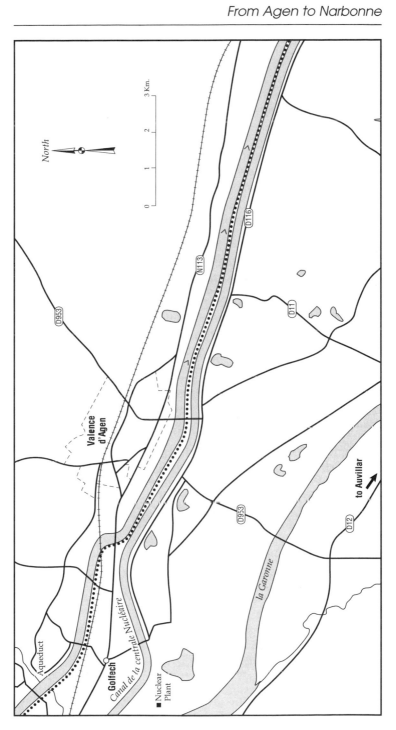

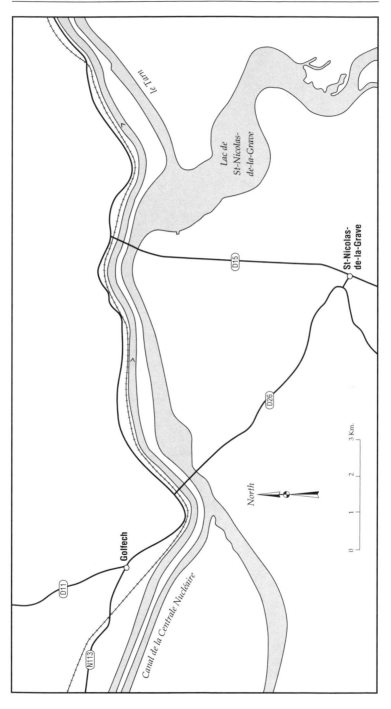

nuclear canal on your right and the canal on your left, a condition that will persist all the way to Moissac. The major market town of Valance d'Agen announces itself with its prominent church steeple on the left bank. The town has built a new marina with picnic facilities to attract mariners and cyclists. The town borrowed its name from Valence, Spain, which also was surrounded by rich agricultural land. Check out its pigeon loft, and if you have laundry to do, there is a nineteenth century wash house right along the canal. A market is held on Tuesday and Saturday mornings.

A worthwhile detour is to Auvillar, just south of Valence. Take D 11 south 2 or 3 miles, and it will transport you into the heart of an Occitan market town of several hundred years ago. Check out its seventeenth century clock tower and sample the fruits of the surrounding countryside.

There is a good, hard-surface pathway on the right bank of the canal leaving Valance d'Agen. Locks come up frequently for a time and you will note that they have been upgraded from the old hand-operated 100-year-old mechanisms to ones that operate with a push-button.

At a point where N 113 and the railroad line come within a stone's throw of the canal and they all take a swing to the left, the Nuclear Canal and the Garonne join, making a large lake to your right. Also joining is the River Tarn, which will be your companion for the rest of the way to Moissac, about 3 miles ahead.

When your path and the canal are crossed by D 15 at the first bridge after Lock 27, Lock Petit Bézy, take a 2-mile detour to your right to the picturesque village of St. Nicholas de la Grave, which clusters around the castle of Richard the Lion Heart. The village was also the birthplace of Antoine Laumet de la Mothe Cadillac, founder of Detroit. His birthplace is an interesting museum.

This region is noted for fruit and nuts, and well-kept orchards and nut groves line both sides of your route. As in most cities touched by the canal, as you enter Moissac, it becomes a major street lined by old brick quays. In Moissac's town center, you continue to have preferred routing, as you approach an old campanile, and soon the busy railroad station.

Moissac is a convenient overnight stop. You can find a hotel with a comfortable room with a shower down the hall for 130 francs with an excellent *prix fixe* meal for 55 francs. The tourist office is tucked away off a courtyard of the old Romanesque cathedral and is supervised by a friendly young lady. The eleventh century Abbaye St. Pierre is worth a visit, even if you have seen a lot of them. Particularly interesting is the ancient inner cloister, perhaps the largest and best example of its kind in Europe. A local specialty: Chasselas table grapes, available in the fall.

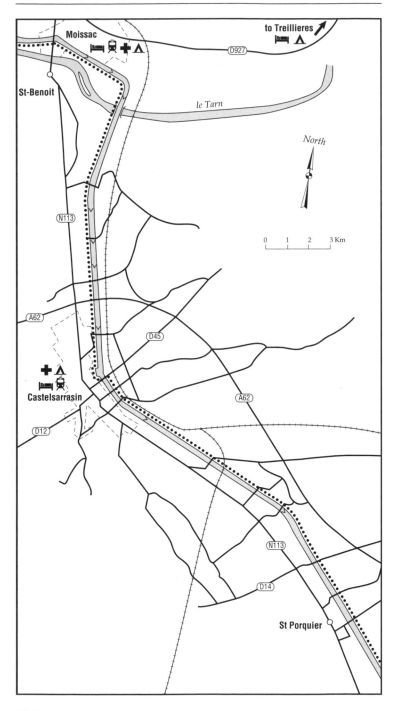

Leaving Moissac, continue riding the right side of the canal. Off to your left, you will pass a number of large playing fields and after that, reminiscent of one of the major reasons for building the canal in the first place, a number of large grain storage silos with pipes once used for loading barges, now hanging mostly unused over the water. About a mile out of town, you come to a large aqueduct, which carries the canal, the towpath, and you high over the River Tarn. The surface of your path is original, round river pebbles, which won't help your outlook on life if your posterior is already tender. The mainline rail tracks from Bordeaux to the Mediterranean remain close to the opposite bank and will keep you company for several miles.

Until you get to Castelsarrasin, locks are dense with only about a half-mile between them. This city's bustling industrial aspect belies its history, which goes back to Neolithic times. The Celts arrived in the sixth century B.C., then the Romans. Remains of a fourteenth century tower are still evident, and in the old section of town are numerous buildings of the 1600s still in use. The town played an important part in the Hundred Years War. Coming into the city you will pass a number of metal working factories. It is a progressive-appearing city with a modern city hall, but it requires a short detour to your right to get to the city center. Market day is Saturday morning.

At Castelsarrasin, cross over to the left bank on the highway bridge and continue along a straight stretch of canal for the next 6 miles. At Montech the original canal engineers had a hill to go over, and they did it by building a dense series of five locks. Recent technology has come to the rescue of commercial and pleasure boaters and the water slope at Montech is worth taking the time to watch in action. There is a short parallel branch of the canal going off to the left. At its beginning is a new lock called a *pente d'eau*. Climbing the hill behind the lock is a massive inclined plane made of concrete. Boats enter the lock, tie up normally, and the entire lock, full of 1,500 tons of water in which boats are floating, travels up the hill via the inclined plane on gigantic rubber-tired wheels. Voila! The boats—lock, water, and all—conquer the hill in one slick operation, eliminating the time-consuming effort of negotiating five conventional locks.

Cyclists get around this complex operation, keeping both the old canal and the new *pente d'eau* bypass on their right. Cross the new section about halfway up the incline and continue up between the old and new sections. At the fourth lock in the five-lock sequence cross the original canal and stay on its right bank. Soon you will pass another canal approaching from the left at right angles. This is a branch canal leading to Montauban.

The 5-mile ride to Montauban is well worth the effort. It is a good example of a French *bastide*, a medieval fortified town,

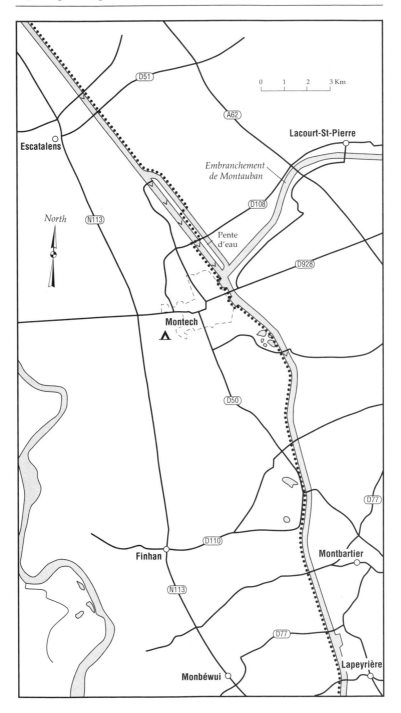

perhaps the earliest type of city planning, with a central square of arcades from which a grid of streets radiates outward. A bridge built across the River Tarn in the fourteenth century is still in use. The painter Ingres was born in Montauban, and he is glorified by one of the most beautiful art museums in France. It is housed in the ancient papal palace. Market day: Saturday.

From Montech for about 10 miles to Grisolles, stay on the right bank through a wide, flat valley with your riding surface reasonably good. The rail line will be your constant companion close on the opposite side of the canal. At Dieupentale most services are offered with a short detour to your right. A small train station serving commuters heading for jobs in Toulouse is across the canal.

Grisolles is another pleasant bedroom community only 15 miles from Toulouse. At the bridge carrying D 52 over the canal, take a left, cross over the bridge, and just past the station you will come to an intersection with the infamous N 113. Fronting on the busy intersection is a modern highway motel with pleasant accommodations and an excellent chef.

A good path leads south from Grisolles, still on the canal's right side. At Lock 9, Emballens, you will pass an ancient mill long disused. Beyond Castelnau d'Estretefonds the towpath becomes a superb, class A surface and your tires sing as you roll along almost effortlessly past modern suburbs and newly electrified locks. Don't be confused by the traffic lights you pass as you approach the locks. They control only the boats approaching the locks, part of a new system meant to enable boaters to operate the locks themselves by pushing a switch and eliminating the need for *éclusiers*.

At Lespinasse you will encounter the first hill you've seen all day. The huffing and puffing will last no more than 100 yards, as you again resume level travel with sure signs of your approach to a great metropolis. Just beyond Fenouillet, a much shrunken River Garonne is visible on your right and in addition to the happy sound of your tires on the excellent pathway, there is the frequent characteristic two-tone whistles of the steady stream of trains heading in and out of Toulouse.

Worried about handling city traffic for the first time in a while? Don't be, just stay with the canal even as country changes to city. There is a large school on your right and among its athletic fields is a well-developed obstacle course for cyclists. Feel sportive? Join the kids. At Lock No. 1, Lalande, it's necessary to take a short detour around a maintenance yard. Keeping the busy superhighway on your right, follow a small road around the yard for a block or two, then swing back to the canal and stay on the right bank along a straight stretch leading to the major canal junction a mile ahead.

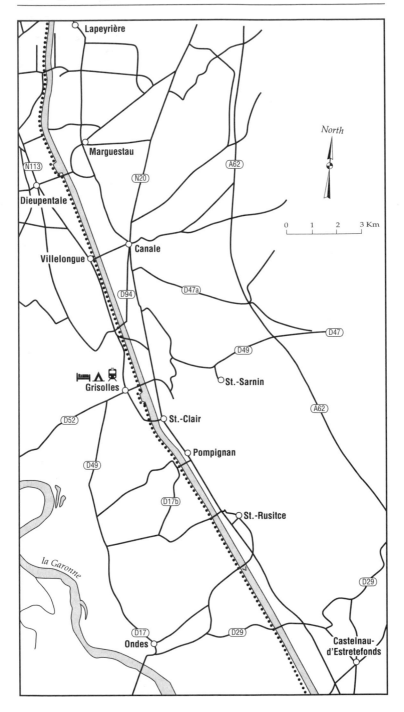

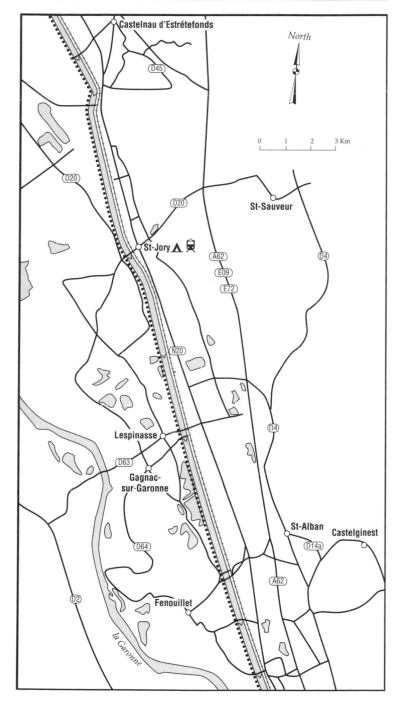

Canal du Midi

At the junction is a turning basin, the Canal Lateral à la Garonne ends, and the Canal du Midi starts at 90 degrees to the left. Just before the intersection, take the old brick bridge over the canal just beyond a nest of barges, *peniches*, then the first bridge over the Canal du Midi to resume your right bank travel.

You pass a new Ibis Motel on the towpath immediately on your right. At the first lock move over to the left bank and continue on that side into the city center, alternately using the main street next to the canal or park paths. In any event, the canal should be kept immediately on your right shoulder. You know you are in the city center when within a few minutes—often faster than the traffic you're accompanying—you arrive in front of the imposing railroad station, the *gare*. As in many principal cities on this route, the canal passes directly in front of the station, where there is also a lock. A new bus station is located to the left of the rail station. Scores of hotels, some deluxe, some commercial, are in the area.

Toulouse is one of France's most important cities, the principal city of the Gascony region and capital of the département of Haute Garonne. It is a bustling, progressive city, center of France's aerospace industry and home of the Airbus and Concorde.

Toulouse is a town not to be overlooked. One of your first stops ought to be the tourist office, located in the *Capitole*, the ancient House of Commons, which dates back to the eleventh century. The only remaining vestige is the *donjon* or tower which houses the tourist office. The facade of the building, which dates to the mid-1700s, is impressive, and behind it is the Hall of the Famous, honoring the city's greats.

Toulouse is known as the "pink city," for the color of the bricks used to construct its many beautiful public buildings.

The Pilgrim's Route, A Worthwhile Detour

The city fathers of Toulouse have a high regard for cyclists, as you will soon experience in your pedaling out of the city along the Canal du Midi on the *Piste Cyclable*. If you are not pressed for time, check in at the tourist office for maps and information on a bike route following the ancient pilgrim route toward the high Pyrenees and Compostelle in Spain.

This route takes you through the southern part of the city and follows generally the valley of the Garonne. The circuit following the tread of millions of medieval Christians is about 100 miles long. Plan two to four days.

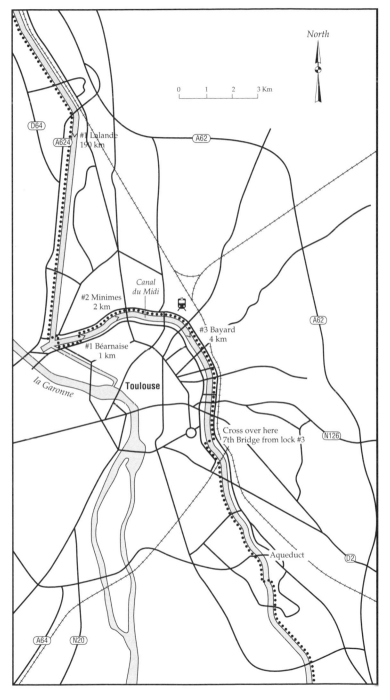

Throughout the centuries, the Basilica of St. Sernin was an important staging point for European pilgrims following the route toward St. Jacques de Compostelle in Spain. It is a jewel of Romanesque architecture.

The city is full of museums, art galleries, and magnificent public gardens, and has a national concert orchestra and a well-regarded summer music festival. Another local attraction is Bernuy's Hotel, a bizarre private home built by a local merchant who, along with the rest of the city, became prosperous in the diemaking trade. After the Middle Ages, Toulouse developed a textile die, intigotine, made from a plant called pastel, and for many decades held a world monopoly. Bernuy's mansion is today a major tourist stop.

Heading out from the city center, continue on the left-hand side of the canal using the street. Within a few blocks in a park-like setting, you will pass a number of one-time *peniches* that now make their living as upscale theme restaurants. Just beyond a small port for pleasure boats called Port St. Sauveur, cross over on the highway bridge to the right bank, where you will pick up a trafficless hard-surfaced pedestrianized roadway that within a short distance announces itself the *Piste Cyclable*, without doubt the most deluxe bicycle route in all of France. It will carry you effortlessly through a number of pleasant villages of the Lauragais, a region that grew rich in the blue dye trade four or five centuries ago.

In many places the original towpath is extant and in better than average shape. It has, however, been succeeded by the well-designed asphalt roadway that continues exclusively for cyclists and walkers through a pleasant park of old trees all the way to the border of the *département*, near Narouze, about 25 miles.

On the border of the city, the canal and the superpath pass over an arterial highway leading into the city from A 62. There are a number of high-rise apartment buildings and large playing fields. Staying on the cycle path is not difficult, as direction signs abound and lead you soon on a cyclist-pedestrian bridge over the canal, to resume travel on the left bank. Don't be surprised to find commuters sharing the pathway with you, briefcases slung over their backs or tucked in a pannier. This kind of travel could give commuting a good name.

The pathway uses an impressive circular rampway to get past a large marina and boatyard. The up-market apartment complex with balconies overlooking yacht slips on the opposite side of the canal could be located in Newport Beach or Fort Lauderdale.

From time to time, the superpathway splits into two divided traffic lanes separated by a line of trees. The canal here becomes quite curvy and particularly beautiful. On the opposite

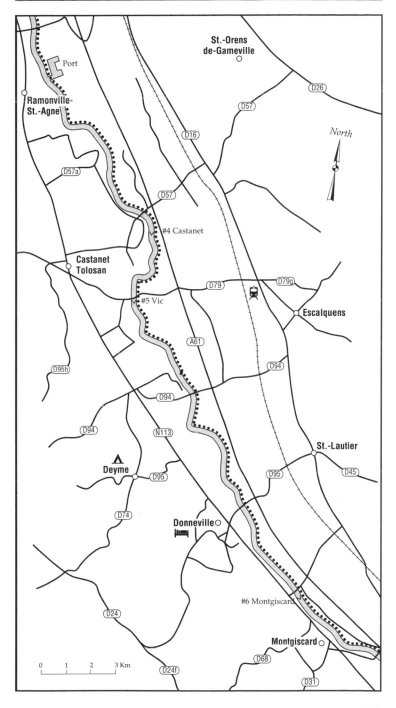

side your eye can't miss the Ile de Galion, a make-believe pirate ship that serves as a restaurant-theme park, complete with swimming pool. If it is time to think of overnight accommodations, just beyond the pirate ship, take the next road heading to the right, where within a quarter-mile you will re-encounter N 113 and a campground. Continuing on N 113 to the left will bring you to the crossroads village of Donneville, which offers an attractive motel/restaurant, L'Enclos. Accommodations are a cluster of individual and distinctive cottages. It's a great place for catching your breath and dining sumptuously.

Regaining the left bank path, you find yourself only a few yards from the busy autoroute A 61, which links Toulouse with Carcassonne, Narbonne, and the sea. The traffic is going a lot faster and with a lot more stress than you on your own super-highway. The pathway is excellent. From time to time, you will encounter local bikers who may be out for a quick five-mile run before supper. Invariably they'll be traveling at speed, decked out in colorful bikers' plumage, and so serious they may not even notice us long-distance plodders.

At regular intervals in this area, you will pass by attractive signs describing where you are and detailing the services available in the neighborhood. And if you are lucky enough to hit this particularly pastoral section in early morning, you'll be enchanted by the morning mist rising off the water, the songs of

Gardouche, once a flourishing center for the commercial barge trade, sleeps in the noonday sun.

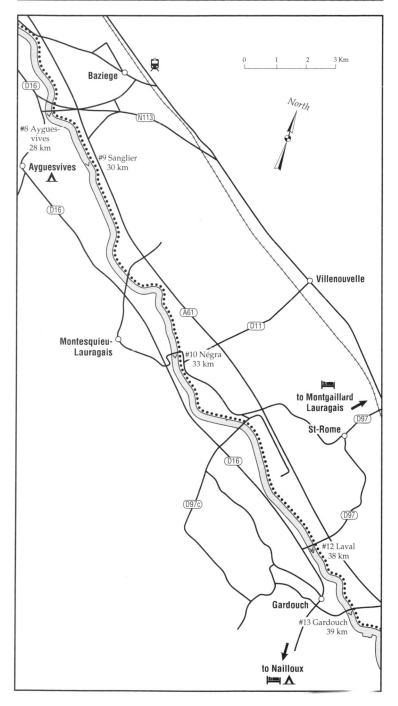

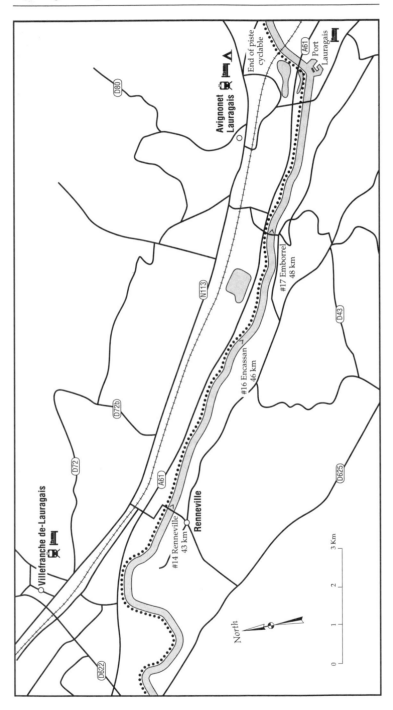

the birds, and the ethereal magic of the scene, which even the nearness of the superhighway can't destroy.

A few hundred yards off to the right of the canal is the red brick village of Ayguesvives, typical of this region. The friezes of its Gothic church may be worth a detour.

Just beyond Sanglier (No. 10), which means wild boar, is a lovely little park with picnic benches, reclining chairs, and even racks for bike parking. The folks that built the *Piste Cyclable* even added guard rails and traffic signs to their bicycle highway. The Château Roquette en Serny rises off to your right, recognized by its broken tower. At the hamlet of Negra, there is a good-sized rental boat fleet headquarters, and at the lock are remains of a once major relay point for the commercial canal traffic, an inn, stables for tow animals, and a chapel.

At the next bridge after the lock at Negra, follow the country road to your left toward St. Rome if for no other reason than to be surprised at the local architecture. At the end of the last century, a much-traveled local nobleman retired to this village and indulged himself in reproducing architecture that he had seen during his travels.

Beyond the lock a few yards there is a major aqueduct, and a couple of miles beyond, a second one, the Aqueduct de Gardouche. The sight of boats crossing high over a river or highway is always a curiosity, but in this region it's a common engineering miracle.

Villefranche de Lauragais, which dates to the thirteenth century, is accessible from the Gardouche lock. Take the road leading off to your left and follow the signs over the superhighway. There is a magnificent fortified wall belfry flanked by octagonal towers. Market day is Friday.

At Gardouche the *piste* takes a well-marked detour from the canal-side for about a quarter-mile. With the cars of the superhighway careening by at upward of 70 miles per hour, it's a great place to philosophize about the pace of your present existence, compared with that of the world beyond, which seems to race by in ignorance of the finer things. A bit farther along on a commanding hill to the right is an old French village with a castle rising in the middle.

Soon you come to another attractive picnic area made primarily for users of the canal and the *piste*, but it has a small annex to serve the highway traffic, too.

With the modern high-speed autoroute so close, it's logical to consider the evolution of travel over the centuries. In the last century the canal was the engineering miracle of its time. Then came the railroad which ribbons this valley about 100 yards away. Then a decade ago came the highway. Now you are riding a new evolution, the ultimate in bicycle pathways.

Moving efficiently and pleasantly past the locks Encassen and Emborrel, you come to the Aqueduct de Radel and you are within sight of the end of the *Piste Cyclable,* the border with the département of Aude and of the canal summit. At the sign marking the end of the pathway, take the bridge over the canal to get to Port Lauragais. This is a wide place in both the waterway and the superhighway, a combination supermarina, rest area, commercial outlet for products of the region, restaurant, hotel, and tribute to Riquet, the canal builder.

To visit Riquet's summit headquarters, continue on the left side of the canal around a couple of sharp curves until you get to Lock Ocean, No. 17, which has been in operation since 1670. You are at Narouze, the canal summit and a place worth taking some time out to explore. At 2,100 feet, it is the highest point on the canal and the point from which all the water needed to operate the locks is gathered and distributed. Amid a magnificent park of huge overhanging trees, Riquet's water basin is still in use, feeding the canal. More than just a canal designer, Riquet envisioned at this point a major new town. Although the canal thrived, the town didn't.

Beyond the park and its lake, follow the signs for the obelisk, a tall monument to the great engineer, built by his family in his memory. After paying your respects to the late M. Riquet, it is best to retrace your steps to Lock Ocean. Use it to cross over to the right side of the canal. Starting out, the path doesn't hold much promise. It is basically one track in the grass, but the surface won't cause any grief. Stay on the right-hand side all the way to Castelnaudary, about 7 miles ahead. The principal problem along unimproved paths like this stretch is tree roots. Care is advised.

At the next bridge you can find villages with most services a short distance in either direction. Le Segala is to the right, Labastide d'Anjou to the left, and on the canal, a small boat marina with telephones, toilets, and other services available without leaving the canal bank. Locks in this section, oddly elliptical in shape, are quite close together, each one in its turn giving you a nice downhill push to the next one. Laurens is a triple lock, giving you a triple boost toward your destination, and the pathway is improving.

Soon the canal breaks out of a forested area, and on every side are huge grain fields as far as you can see. The only shade in sight is what you are enjoying, the wonderfully mature trees that line every canal in France. Soon advertising signs reveal the gastronomic specialty of the region, *cassoulet.* It is a rich stew featuring white beans, pork, goose, mutton, and sausages and in Castelnaudary you are hard put to find a menu that doesn't offer it. As you approach this lovely old canal port, the towpath

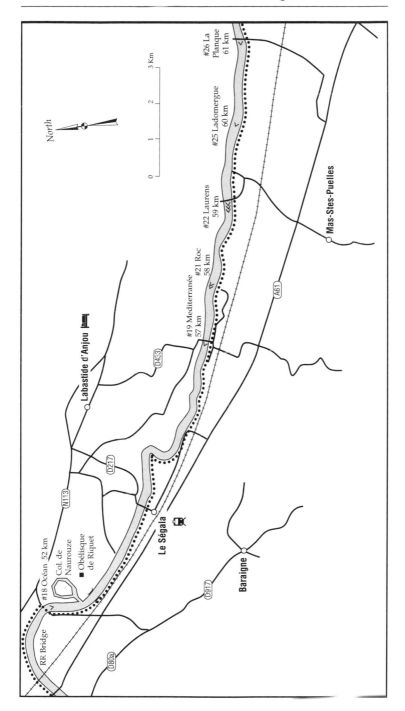

North

0   1   2   3 Km

#26 La
Planque
61 km

#25 Ladomergue
60 km

#22 Laurens
59 km

#21 Roc
58 km

#19 Mediterranée
57 km

#18 Océan 52 km

Col. de
Naurouze

■ Obélisque
de Riquet

RR Bridge

Labastide d'Anjou

Le Ségala

Baraigne

Mas-Stes-Puelles

N113

D217

D433

A61

D917

D80a

greatly improves and leads you down a park-like *allée* into the town center.

On your right fronting the canal is a very attractive hostelry, the Hôtel du Canal. There are other hotels around the station a block or two to the right. More hotels are found up the imposing Cours de la République, an attractive tree-lined street leading up the hill past the post office and the town hall. On the right about halfway up the street is a bicycle repair shop. At the top of the street to the left is the tourist office and across the street a laundromat.

At Castelnaudary, cross to the left bank and keep the large turning basin with the rental boat operation on your right. Here the towpath has a lovely hard surface and you have a good downhill glide as you pass a triple lock. Two restaurants featuring regional specialties front the path here. The downhill slope continues past densely positioned locks and while the hard surface that started out is now gravel, it is excellent and allows you to shift into the highest gear and take advantage of the rare downhill slope.

At Lock Peyruque (No. 29), a sign cautions that the maximum speed for cyclists is 10K (7 miles per hour) in front of the lockkeeper's house. The lockkeeper at La Criminelle (No. 30) is a fervent fan of M. Riquet. The house and lock are decorated with memorabilia of the engineer's life. For a short run the towpath, still on the left side, is a country road, but after the Aqueduct de Treboul and the lock of the same name, the path becomes a category C. If you suffer from the cyclists' malady called keister kramps, the rough surface won't improve things.

As you ride along with few signs of civilization, you are conscious that here nature is in charge. There is a lot of scuttling among the dry bushes and reeds, probably made by lizards or rabbits. There are also a lot of splashes in front of you, some of them remarkably substantial. One wonders the size of the beasts that cause it. Often fish jump in the water at your right elbow and herons and swans land and take off constantly.

At the next bridge beyond Treboul (No. 31) just beyond a small boat mooring area you can take D 213 to the left for Villepinte, a small village of the Langueduc, where most services are available. At Bram the lockkeeper has indicated with signs that cyclists should take a small detour behind his house. No problem. At the next bridge, Highway D 4 leads to the right to Bram, which has a railroad station and is a regional center. To attract the pleasure boat market, the town has recently widened the canal and installed a small boat mooring.

Just beyond the Aqueduct de Rebenti and the railroad bridge, the towpath ends abruptly. Take the D 33 bridge to the right bank then a small country road that parallels the canal to

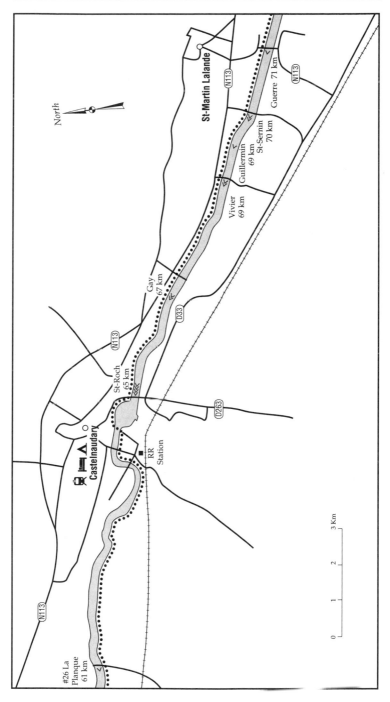

North

St-Martin Lalande

N113

Guerre 71 km

N113

St-Sernin 70 km

Guillermin 69 km

Vivier 69 km

Gay 67 km

D33

N113

St-Roch 65 km

D263

Castelnaudary

RR Station

3 Km

0   1   2

#26 La Planque 61 km

N113

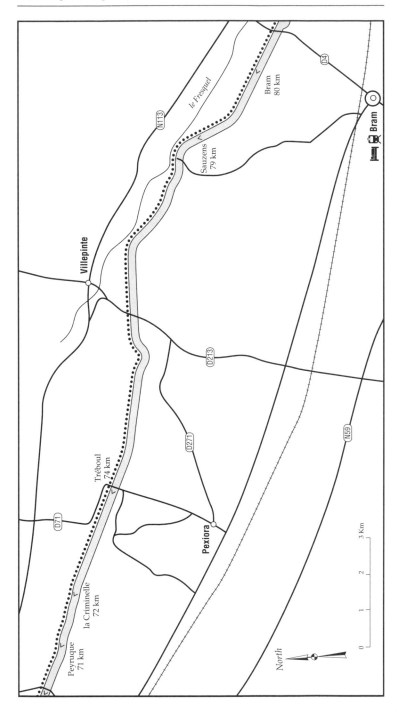

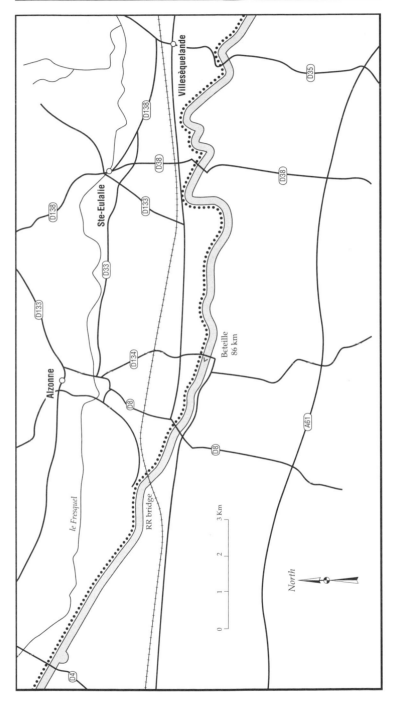

Lock Beteille (No. 35), where the left bank towpath resumes. Here you are about 10 miles from Carcassonne, and you are reminded of another benefit of canal cycling: cyclists approaching major cities are not confronted by ugly advertising signs as they are when approaching by highway. Instead, almost invariably, what had been the original unimproved towpath becomes a hard-surfaced roadway flanked by benches and parks.

After passing the Aqueduct de Lespitalet, the canal goes through a number of twists and turns around the village of Villesquelande. Beyond the tiny port at Sauzens, cyclists face a small challenge. Here the towpath becomes a single track requiring a bit of care, when the hill on the left forces the path perilously close to the canal bank on the right. It's only a temporary peril, but the towpath doesn't improve in this area until you get to Lalande (No. 37).

At the next bridge beyond Sauzens, take the highway to the left. Within a half mile you will pass a large wine cooperative with a well-decorated and stocked wine cellar.

Here in Pezens the village church, la Madeleine, is located in the middle of the highway.

As you enter Carcassonne you pass a large builders' yard and other commercial and industrial plants. As you get into the city itself, abandon the towpath and take to the parallel street. Both the street and the canal will take you into the city center. As in Toulouse, the canal passes directly in front of the rail station and the most prominent business at this point is a McDonald's.

Carcassonne has been a citadel and center of southwestern France since its founding in the thirteenth century by Saint Louis. The old city with its medieval ramparts is one of the major tourist destinations of the country. More than two million people visit each year. In the eighteenth century, Carcassonne grew rich in the wine and textile trade. Today it continues a major commercial center as well as a tourist attraction.

Some ancient travel writer once said that if Paris is worth a mass, Carcassonne is worth three days. A visit to the old medieval city ringed by 2 miles of walls and 52 towers is an absolute must. People still live and work within the old walls, and excellent hotels, restaurants, galleries, and craft shops are found there. Wander the ancient cobbled streets and feel you are one with Lancelot and King Arthur.

If you are a lover of the bubbly wines, head south from Carcassonne on D 118 and pedal for the village of Limoux, about 13 miles away, home of an excellent sparkling wine that some experts think is as good as champagne. Ask for a glass of Blanquette de Limoux.

Leaving Carcassonne, it's best to take to the edge of the two-lane highway that flanks the canal on the right side. Carbon

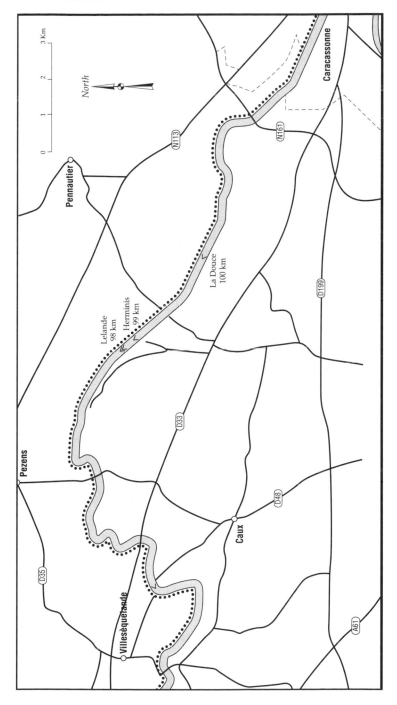

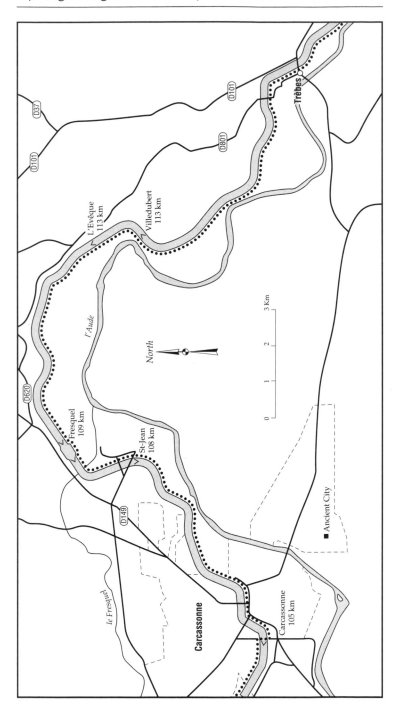

monoxide fumes and the stress of passing cars, trucks, and buses will be with you only until the first lock, St. Jean, where you can find the original towpath again. The path is excellent here with a dense line of cypresses providing shade, beauty, and an effective windscreen. You pass over a tributary to the River Aude then come to a quadruple lock at Fresquel, which is controlled by an *éclusier* sitting in something that looks like the precursor of an airport control tower.

Don't be fooled into taking the hard-surfaced country road that parallels the single track towpath. The road deviates soon, and it's best to stay on the right-hand towpath. The pathway winds its narrow way alongside the canal amongst tall reeds. Actually the surface may not have been improved since Riquet's time, but it is still easily negotiated and remarkably smooth. For several miles you will pass through a forest where the only sign of humanity is the canal and the path you are following. Nothing here has been done to deter the densely overhanging branches of the forest, and the tall reeds you are passing through make no space for more than one bike at a time. It may be the most interesting segment of the entire route.

At Lock l'Evêque (No. 44) you can follow the small country road to the right or stay with the towpath. The path widens here and the surface is good, but there is a persisting problem: tree roots. From time to time without warning a tree root, sometimes a foot high, snakes out from the row of very old plane trees. In some places it's necessary to get off and walk to avoid a broken wheel.

After Lock Villedubert (No. 45), stay on the little country road until it ends up in a peasant's farmyard and you can regain the right-hand towpath once again. The ancient who was responsible for planting the plane trees stopped here, and big tree roots are no longer a problem as you approach the market town of Trèbes in high gear over an excellent surface.

Grapes are a major crop in this area, and off to your right are the vineyards of Corbières and beyond the foothills of the Pyrenees. To the north is an equally important wine area, the Minervois. The picturesque village of Berriac with its squared-off steeple shows up off to your right, and there is a narrow medieval bridge on your left. The excellent pathway continues to the Aqueduct d'Orbeil, which was built by Riquet's successor, Vauban, in 1686. Trèbes is an attractive village that has made its canal front an appealing place for pleasure boaters to stop. At the triple lock, on the far side of town, you might want to check out the Auberge du Moulin, which offers accommodations and a good meal.

The pathway, still on the right, continues in class A condition. A working château, St. Julia, with a big octagonal tower shaded

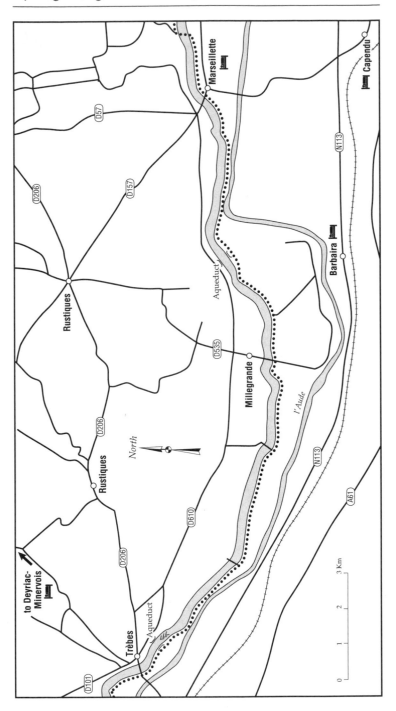

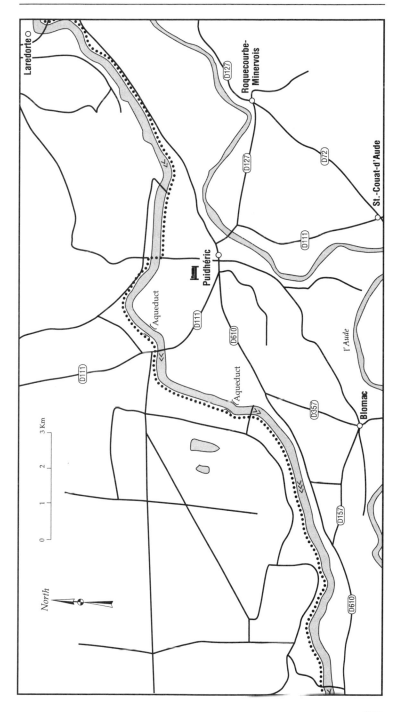

by very old pines, is on the opposite side of the canal, accessible via an ancient bridge with rotting planks. Its principal business, wine, is easily identifiable. Past the hamlets of Millepetit and Millegrand the way continues in good condition. Here the surrounding countryside has become more hilly and the canal makes its way through the hills by deep cuts. At Marseillette you pass a major two-lane highway and a wine cooperative with some excellent wines. In season there are booths selling regional produce and there are crafts for sale at the lockkeeper's house.

At Marseillette cross over to the left-hand bank and until you get to the triple lock of Fonfile (No. 48), the towpath and the canal will be isolated from the outside world by steep banks. From Aiguille you might want to diverge on D 111 to the medieval village of Puichéric. Head up the winding, narrow streets toward the church tower and pass by the walls of an eleventh century *château* burned down in the fourteenth century by the Black Prince. The people of Puichéric live among walls that haven't changed in 900 years.

From Aiguille on the canal, a left will take you in a couple of miles to the Château de St. Annay, which offers excellent meals and its own wines. From Aiguille, which means needle, the towpath following the right bank should be your choice. Next town is Laredorte, which the canal bypasses in a big swinging turn to its south. Laredorte's claim to fame is an old château and a lot of wine.

A restaurant seeking business from folks using the canal is happily accessible. Just beyond the town is a very impressive old aqueduct, Argentdouble, with a built-in valve obviously used to control canal levels. Cross to the left bank just before you come to the aqueduct, but only briefly. At the farm bridge just before you come to Joarre (No. 52), return to the right bank.

The path here is Class A for a short distance, interrupted by the construction of a good-sized basin that looks like an investment gone sour. It is almost empty of boats and the banks are overgrown. It's necessary to use back roads to detour around it. Civilization seems closer now, and soon you arrive in the attractive little village of Homps, a good place to provision or take a rest stop. Homps was civilized as far back as the third century B.C. and has been a prosperous river and canal port for the shipment of Corbières wine for centuries. Wine merchants and co-ops still flourish here but the commercial port has become a busy stop for pleasure boats. Among its riches is a ninth century chapel and a tower of the Knights of Malta.

Within a quarter mile of Homps the canal takes an abrupt 90-degree turn to the right. On an aqueduct you pass over a tributary to the close-by River Aude and pass through a very attractive

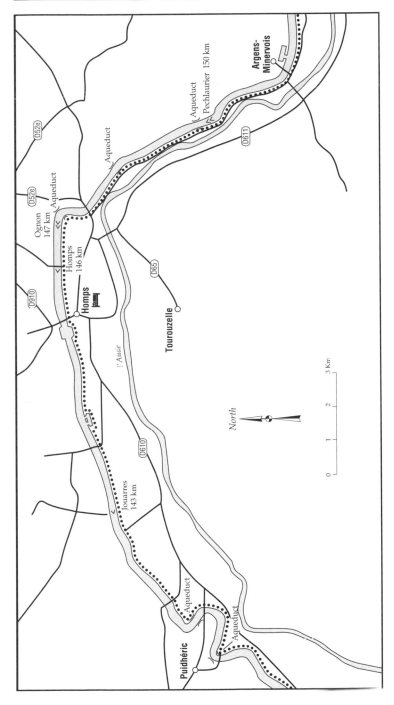

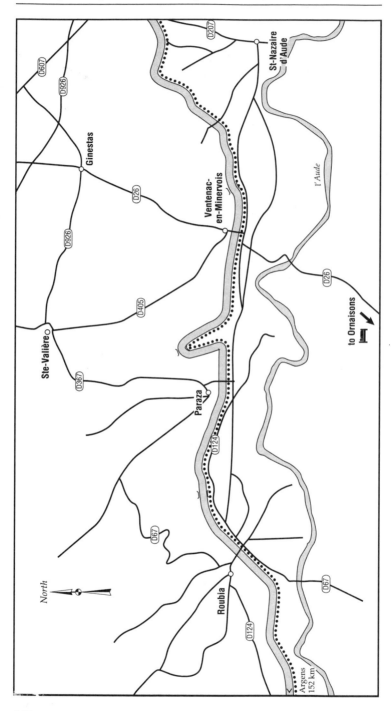

waterside area where the canal takes several other sharp turns. At the picturesque canalside restaurant, l'Escale, outside diners have a rushing stream almost at their feet, while they watch the busy canal activity directly in front of them.

After passing by a number of ancient canal buildings, take the country road that parallels the right-hand towpath to Pechlaurier, No. 55, a double lock where you regain the towpath on the right. At Argens-Minervois the towers of a castle in ruins dominate the entire village. Most services are available here.

Your growing proximity to the Mediterranean is starting to be evident: the characteristic smell of the pines, olive and palm trees, bougainvillea, and the plaited reed fences used as windbreaks to protect kitchen gardens against the mistral winds. At Roubia the town has laid out picnic tables in a small park for your use. After passing by Paraza, the canal takes a sharp oxbow to the left and at the U-turn passes over the Répoudre River on a single aqueduct span of 11 meters, reputed to be the oldest canal aqueduct in the world.

If, however, you've seen enough aqueducts and you're eager to find a bed for the night, follow D 124 on the right of the canal, bypass the oxbow, and arrive at the village of Ventenac-en-Minervois, whose silhouette from the canalside has an interesting juxtaposition of ancient battlements and modern stainless-steel wine tanks.

A great place to stop for the night is Le Somail, a tiny village and wide place in the canal whose past was closely linked with the canal traffic. During the canal's heyday, Le Somail was a transfer point for packet boat passengers. Today it has a small but bustling port, a strange-looking, but hospitable *chambre d'hôte*, and an up-market, gourmet restaurant plus a few interesting craft shops. Run out of reading matter? The village has a very extensive secondhand book shop.

If your destination is Narbonne, the Midi for you ends about a mile south of Le Somail, where the Embranchement de la Nouvelle takes you on a 90-degree turn to the right, as the Midi continues on toward Béziers. Following the straight Embranchement you continue on the right side, using a canal bank roadway for 2 miles to its end at Salleles-d'Aude, a busy commercial center. At this point the canal towpath route becomes complicated by its intersection with the River Aude and the beginning of the short Canal de la Robine. It is best to abandon the canal here and take to highway D 1118 in the direction of Cuxac d'Aude. In the center of this busy suburban town, several excellent bakeries feature a foot-long delicious pastry filled with cheese. Take Route D 13 to the right, pass over the River Aude on the far side of town, and continue toward Narbonne for about a mile. You will meet the Canal de la Robine at Lock Raonelle.

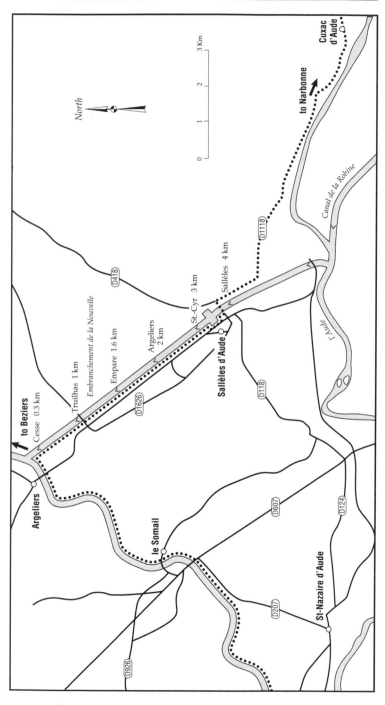

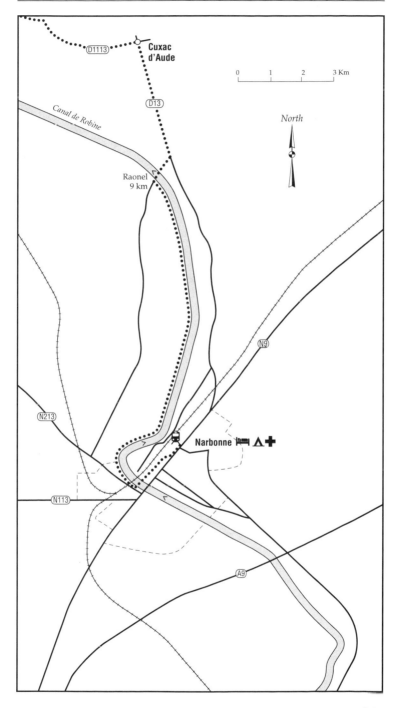

This is a pretty little lock, which the lockkeeper has made even prettier with gardens and his love of music. Don't be surprised to be met by a full orchestra playing operatic arias over excellent reproduction equipment. If you can bear to tear yourself away, cross to the right side of the canal here and pedal off the last 3 miles to Narbonne through a tunnel made by the branches of huge overhanging plane trees. (Note: don't forget to watch out for the roots.) As you enter the city past a huge petroleum tank farm on your left, you go around the Lock Gua, then using city streets and the parking lots of an old people's home, regain the canal side. When the canal meets a large boulevard, Boulevard Frederic Mistral, in the center of town, leave the canal and take the bridge to your left. By following it a few blocks you will come to the railroad station.

Narbonne has very ancient roots, which go back at least to the seventh century B.C. when it was first colonized by the Phoenicians and later the Greeks. In the days of Caesar, it was the leading Roman colony outside Italy, a major Mediterranean port and for a time the capital of Gaul.

If you continue on the canalside you will encounter the Merchants' Bridge in the town center. In Roman times it carried the ancient classical highway Via Domitia over the Roman-engineered grandfather of the present canal. On Sunday mornings, a huge market is held in a modern covered building fronting the canal. Merchants who can't be accommodated inside have hundreds of stalls surrounding the area and the patronage is dense.

South of the city the canal traverses a long narrow isthmus for about 12 miles to the final lock, where it meets the sea at Port la Nouvelle. This is an area of marshes and tidal flats full of deer and waterfowl. It's the end of the line. Nice going—you made it to saltwater.

Chapter 19

Canal Lateral à la Garonne and Canal du Midi—Accommodations

Hotels, Guest Houses, Campgrounds, Phone Numbers, and Other Useful Information

Note: Communities are listed in order geographically from Agen toward the end of the canal by the sea. Numbers following hotel and guest house listings indicate number of rooms; those following campground listings indicate number of campsites. Number following community name is ZIP code. Stars are the government luxury rating system of France.

Agen 47006 (Market: daily)

There are more than 25 hotels in Agen. For a complete list and other information on this fascinating city, write: Office de Tourisme, 107 Boulevard Carnot, B.P. 207, 47006 Agen.

Camping		
Château LaMothe d'Allot	100	53 68 33 11
Youth Hostel	60	53 66 18 98
Tourist Office		53 66 14 14

Bon Encontre 47000

Hotel		
le Parc	10	53 96 17 75
Guest House		
Château de Labatut	2	53 96 26 24
Camping		
Municipal	50	56 96 61 78

Valance d'Agen 82400
(Market: Tuesday and Saturday morning)

Hotels		
de France		63 39 63 31
l'Etape		63 29 10 50
Tout Va Bien		63 39 54 83
Guest House		
Mme Yvonne Lauzin	2	63 29 07 49
Camping		
Municipal**	33	63 39 54 07
Hospital		63 39 50 67

Auvillar 82340

Hotels	
de l'Horlage	63 39 91 61
Château St. Roch***	63 95 95 22
Tourist Office	63 39 57 33

St. Nicholas de la Grave 82340 (Market: Monday morning)

Hotels		
les Escales		63 94 80 21
Auberge de la Garonne		63 04 06 82
Guest House		
Christiane Valette		63 95 59 15
Camping		
du Plan d'Eau	42	63 95 93 92

Moissac 82200

Hotels		
le Luxembourg*		63 04 00 27
de la Poste		63 04 01 47
Pont Napoleon*		63 04 01 55
au Chapin Fin**		63 04 04 22
Relais Auvergnat		63 04 02 58
Marengo		63 04 81 13
Auberge des Cretes de Pignols		63 04 04 04
Lamagistere		63 04 06 82
la Garonne		63 04 06 82
le Relais		63 39 77 84
Camping		
le Bidounet***	140	63 32 29 96
Hospital		63 04 67 00
Tourist Office		63 04 01 85

Castelsarrasin 82100 (Market: Saturday morning)

Hotels		
Felix**	10	63 32 14 97
Artel**	35	63 95 03 03
Moderne**		63 32 30 10
de Commerce*	15	63 32 30 83
Relais des Deux Mers	12	63 32 30 88
de la Gare		63 32 21 00
des Deux Ponts	12	63 32 34 45
Marceillac**	12	63 32 30 10
la Promenade		63 32 30 72
Guest House		
les Dantous	5	63 32 26 95
Camping		
de Trecasses-sur-Garonne	33	63 32 30 37
Hospital		63 32 88 00
Tourist Office		63 32 14 88

La Française 82130

Hotel		
le Fin Gourmet**		63 65 89 55
Guest House		
Guffoy		63 65 84 46
Camping		
Vallée des Loisirs***	56	63 65 89 69

Montech 82700

Camping		
Municipal*	30	63 64 82 44

Grisolles 82170

Hotel		
Relais des Garrigues		
Camping		
Aquitaine***	40	63 67 33 22

St. Jory 31790

Camping		
Lamarque		61 35 53 97

Toulouse

Toulouse has scores of hotels and points of interest to choose from. For a complete list, contact the Toulouse Tourist Office, Tel. 61 11 02 22.

Camping			
de Rupe***		285	61 70 07 35
la Bouriette**		73	61 49 64 46

Deyme 31450

Camping			
Les Violettes**		80	61 81 72 07
Tourist Office			61 81 71 93

Donneville 31450

Hotel			
l'Enclos		8	61 81 90 84
Tourist Office			61 81 96 60

Aiguesvives 31450

Camping			
les Peupliers*			61 81 11 11
Tourist Office			61 81 92 57

Montgaillard-Lauragais

Hotel			
Hostellerie du Chef Jean**		13	61 81 62 55

Nailloux 31560

Hotels			
du Pastel**		25	61 81 46 61
le Relais		6	61 81 30 55
Camping			
le Parc de la Thesauque***			61 81 34 67
Aire Naturel			61 81 34 98
Tourist Office			61 81 30 20

Villefranche-de-Lauragais 31290 (Market: Friday)

Hotels			
de France**		18	61 81 62 17
des Voyageurs**		18	61 27 02 27
Auberge de la Pradelle**		7	61 81 60 72
du Lauragais**		21	61 27 00 76
la Route de Pastel			61 81 62 11
Tourist Office			61 27 20 94

Avignonet Lauragais 31290

Hotels

l'Obelesque*		61 81 63 76
la Couchee**		61 27 17 12
la Pergola*		61 81 63 54
le Pilori*		61 27 12 47

Camping

Municipal de Piqueraisin	25	61 81 63 67

Tourist Office   61 81 63 67

La Bastide d'Anjou 11320

Hotel

le Grilladou**	14	68 60 11 63

Castelnaudary 11400 (Market on Monday)

Hotels

de France et Notre Dame***	17	68 23 10 18
du Canal**	33	68 94 05 05
le Clos de Simeon**	31	68 94 01 20
Grand Hotel Fourcade*	12	68 23 02 08
Centre		68 23 25 95
le Siècle		68 23 27 23

Camping

Chemin du Ferie		68 94 11 28

Carcassonne 11000 (Market on Tuesday, Thursday, Saturday)

Carcassonne has scores of hotels and points of interest to choose from. For a complete list, contact the Carcassonne Tourist Office, Tel. 68 25 07 04.

Camping

de la Cité	250	68 25 11 77

Youth Hostels

la Cité	120	68 25 23 16

Trèbes 11800 (Market on Wednesday)

Hotels

la Gentilhommière**	31	68 78 74 74
Andalousie		68 78 88 88

Camping

Chemin de la Lande		68 78 61 75

Barbaira 11800

Guest House

Mme Kavos		68 79 06 91

Marseillette 11800
Hotel
la Muscadelle**   9   68 79 20 90

Capendu 11700
Hotel
le Top du Roulier   68 79 03 60

Puichéric 11700
Guest House
Château St. Aunay   5   68 43 72 20

Homps 11200
Hotels
le Clos des Muscats***   10   68 91 38 50
de la Gare   68 91 38 50

Le Somail 11120
Guest House
Chez Bernaleu   68 46 16 02

Narbonne 11100 (Market on Sunday, Tuesday, Thursday)
Narbonne has scores of hotels and points of interest to choose
from. For a complete list, contact the Narbonne Tourist Office,
Tel. 68 65 15 60.
Guest House
Chemin Bas Razimbaud   4   68 32 52 06
Camping
Les Mimosas***   160   68 49 03 72
Les Floralys**   30   68 32 65 65
Roche Gris**   130   68 41 75 41

Port la Nouvelle 11210 (Market on Wednesday, Saturday)
Hotels
la Méditerranée   68 48 03 08
le Beau Rivage   68 48 83 27
du Port   68 48 01 76
Camping
CôteVermeille***   334   68 48 05 80

Chapter 20

It's a State of Mind

How to Get There and Back

Dijon, the start of your explorations of Burgundy, has air service linking it with Paris and other major cities, but it is far less expensive and as efficient to use the excellent train service, usually less than two hours from Paris. From the Gare de Lyon, trains, many nonstop TGV, leave about every half-hour during normal travel hours. Your trek through Burgundy is never far from the Paris-Dijon rail line. Many nearby towns offer service in the event you need to abort before you get to the end of the route. LaRoche-Migennes, where the canal ends, offers excellent commuter service to Paris (about an hour).

Your Route North

The fabled land of Burgundy starts not far from the commuter communities south of Paris. But there is little about Burgundy that evokes the bustle of the metropolis. It is a region of rugged, forest-covered mini-mountains, gently rolling hills, wild, tumbling rivers, and luxuriant valleys. Sprinkled here and there, sometimes seemingly without reason, are the magnificent remains of a rich and varied culture that reaches back through unwritten history to man's earliest steps upon the planet.

Burgundy, for eons, has played gracious host to visitors from all over the world. But still more thousands travel through it en route to other, more sophisticated locales. Burgundy finds herself, as she always has, on vital routes to elsewhere. In the old days she straddled the tin, salt, and amber caravan routes. Later it was the water routes plied by the shallow-drafted river boats and, beginning with the seventeenth century, the canal barges. Today coddled passengers on the TGV rail line look hungrily at Burgundian scenery racing past at 200 miles per hour as they

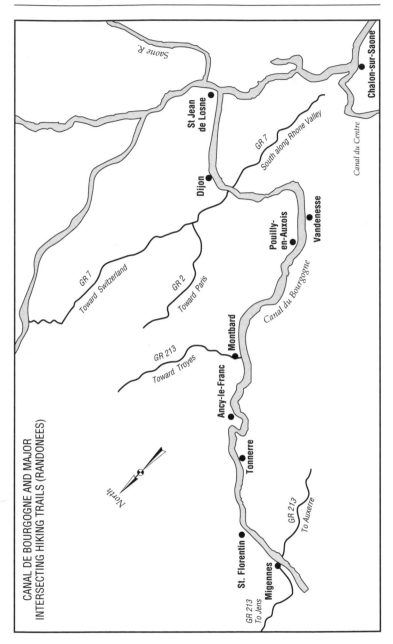

CANAL DE BOURGOGNE AND MAJOR
INTERSECTING HIKING TRAILS (RANDONEES)

hurry to the beaches of Provence, the ski resorts of the Alps, or the nightclubs of Paris.

The smart ones get off at Dijon to sample the special charms of Burgundy. We will, too, as we prepare to follow what many say is France's most beautiful canal route. Burgundy has been called an *état d'esprit*, a state of mind. It is also a name for a region that consists of four *départements:* Nièvre and Saône-et-Loire, which are south and west of our canal route, the Côte d'Or (Gold Coast) of which Dijon is the capital, and Yonne in the far north end of our ride. Burgundy is a little larger than Maryland, but has about one-quarter of Maryland's population, which highlights one of the region's persistent woes, depopulation.

Burgundy may have people problems at only 50 per square mile, about half that of the rest of the country, but it doesn't have a shortage of water. It is the spawning ground of many of France's most important rivers. It is said that of six drops of rain that fall on this land, two will find their way to the English Channel, two will end in the Mediterranean, and two will flow to the Atlantic.

The combination of rivers and a geography that puts Burgundy strategically between major markets led to the establishment of one of the world's most highly developed water transportation systems. Between Paris and the Mediterranean, one can choose from four different river-canal routes, all of which at least partially pass through Burgundy.

The hills and rivers and the canals that connect them have made Burgundy into a cultural patchwork quilt. Each hamlet and village is separated from its neighbors by its own special and fascinating heritage. The houses in one village will all be built of a special type of limestone, while only a few miles away the houses will be built of brick and timber. It all adds up to a fascinating variety that will follow you as you ride to the far end of the canal.

A Bit of History

The remnants of human history go as far back in Burgundy as anywhere in the world. Excavations at Azé and Solutré, a short distance south of Dijon, prove that Cro-Magnon man inhabited this area 30,000 years ago. The Greeks and the Etruscans also passed through regularly during the Iron Age and built hill forts to guard their trade routes. Then the Romans came, conquered, and stuck around long enough to leave a rich treasure of artifacts. In 52 B.C., Julius Caesar consolidated his conquest of Gaul by winning a decisive battle with Vercingetorix at Alésia. Your canalside route will take you within an arrow shot of this important battlefield.

The roads the Romans built over the next 400 years to handle trade in salt, tin, amber, and copper are, in many places, the foundations of the high-speed superhighways that cross the Burgundy of today.

Burgundy gets its name from an island, then called Burgundholm in the Baltic Sea off Sweden, from where came an early group of immigrants during the declining years of Roman occupation. Burgundia grew and came to include what is now Geneva, Avignon, Lyon, and Dijon, but it didn't last long as wave after wave of Dark Ages opportunists swept in. These included first the Ostrogoths, then the Moors from Spain, and, in the eighth and ninth centuries, the Norse and the Magyars.

In this part of the world, things only began to settle down when monastic orders started springing up around the countryside. The Benedictines were very active. Besides developing a highly organized system of monasteries, in Cluny they built a gigantic church, the largest in the world until the construction of St. Peter's in Rome about four centuries later. Visit Cluny and what remains of this ancient shrine, only a short detour from your canal path.

Perhaps as important to Burgundy was the rise of the Cistercians, a religious sect whose members opposed what they sensed was Christianity's partnership with materialism. Saint Bernard, a native son, was one of its prime movers.

"For God's sake," he wrote, "if men are not ashamed of these follies, why at least do they not shrink from their expense."

The bare-bones Cistercians built no-fringe monasteries, "simple workshops for prayer," all over Burgundy in the tenth and eleventh

Some of the bike trails will take you through cities such as Dijon.

centuries, adding stability and organization to the land. The monks concentrated on stock breeding, commercial fishing, forestry, wine-making, mining, and smelting. Incidentally, in the process they invented the cam shaft. Saint Bernard's headquarters was at the Cistercian monastery at Fontenay, which is today preserved as the pre-eminent example of the sect's lifestyle. It is close to your route through the northern part of the region and is worth a visit.

In the end it was success that did the Cistercians in. Their decline started when their monasteries, which included huge estates stretching from Russia to Ireland, started being as comfortable as everybody else's. The Crusades didn't start in large metropolitan centers like Paris or London. Two of them, the Second, promoted by Saint Bernard, and the Third, by Richard the Lion-Hearted, were started from the religious center of Vézelay, about 20 miles off your route. Vézelay is today listed as a World Heritage site, but its influence as a religious center was quashed several centuries ago, when an Avignon pope claimed its venerated relics of Mary Magdalene were a fraud, that the real relics were elsewhere.

All of this ecclesiastical activity is proof of the spirituality of the Burgundians. It continues today. But it isn't all Christian. At Dettey is the largest Buddhist monastery in Europe, while at Taizé is a large and flourishing Islamic theological seminary.

Fame, influence, and wealth came to Burgundy in the 1300s when it was known as the Valois Duchy. At its peak it was the largest country in Europe, roughly five times its present size. It stretched to the channel coast and included much of Belgium, Holland, and Luxembourg. It all started with Phillippe the Bold and his heirs, all flaunting wonderful adjectives—Jean the Fearless, Phillippe the Good, and finally Charles the Rash. Charles should have been less rash. He died in a battle with the Swiss near Nancy in 1477, and the dreams of continuing greatness for Burgundy died with him.

From that point Burgundy's individuality took a back seat to the Kingdom of France, of which it became a subservient part. But you only have to wander the picturesque streets and alleys of Dijon to relive the magnificence of Burgundy's greatest hour.

In 1940 it took the German armies only five days to occupy Burgundy, but keeping it took a lot longer. Burgundy was a hot bed of the resistance for the next five years.

Burgundy Today

Dijon and the Côte d'Or have always been Burgundy's undisputed heart. Ever since 1850, Dijon has been a major rail center and today it is an important stop for the TGV heading out of Paris for Geneva (it is only 70 miles from the Swiss border) and for Lyon and the Mediterranean.

The country through which you'll be passing is pastoral, un-hurried, and not greatly changed over the centuries. About 30 percent of it is in woodland, which still shelters wild boar, deer, and buzzards. For part of the time you'll share valleys with a modern highway and the rail line with the fastest trains in the world hurrying by. But not to worry—they don't seem to affect the pace of things along your track.

Much of the stone to build modern Paris came from quar-ries, which will flank your path near Auxonne. Almost all of it went there by canal barge.

Today the region exports a wide diversity of products: steel, electronics, pottery, accordions, and harmonicas. The largest poker chip factory in the world is located here.

In Burgundy, *châteaux* and manor houses have a functional, rather than decorative design. Many were built in isolated areas far from villages or major roads. Even more enchantment is added to your ride when you round a bend and come face-to-face with six or seven centuries of family history. Investigate further; the family may sell you a ticket to their private museum. Or bet-ter still, it may be your most memorable overnight stopping place.

Famous Burgundian sons include Gustave Eiffel, Nicéphore Niepce, the inventor of photography, and Pierre Athanase LaRusse, compiler of the French dictionary.

Wines

Mention Burgundy anywhere in the world, and it evokes a mind's-eye picture of fine wine served with an exquisite meal. One of the region's enthusiastic wine hucksters wrote that drinking a superior Burgundy "is like having an orgasm in one's mouth and nose at the same time." There are no fewer than 112 different vintages that can legally call themselves Burgundy. Their boosters are legion, arbitrarily defensive, believing no oth-er wine in the world compares.

Burgundy's most famous vineyards are south of Dijon and your route, but close to the other end, you will pass within a few miles of another famous name, Chablis. The four communes that can legally use that important name are spread over chalky hills between Tonnerre and Auxerre, about 10 miles to the west of the canal.

Other famous Burgundy vineyards, Beaujolais, Maconnais, Mercurey, Côtes de Nuits, and Beaune, lie to the west of the riv-er Saône south of Dijon.

Burgundian Specialties

Burgundy is almost as famous for its food offerings as for its wines. Restaurants are said to have more stars than anywhere

---

Wine Tips

Some tips the experts would like you to remember when serving good wines:
- —Never drink a wine just off the press; let it rest.
- —When serving two white wines or several reds with dinner, always serve the lightest first, winding up with the most full-bodied last.
- —Meals should begin with a white wine served chilled (43 to 50 degrees F) with seafood.
- —Red wine should be served with meat and cheese and at room temperature.
- —Pour old wines carefully; don't bend.

---

outside of Paris. In Sens, in the north of the region, some traditional eateries feature tables with carved indentations in their table tops to accommodate their patrons' bellies.

Here are some specialties you shouldn't overlook:

Parsleyed or raw ham; *escargots de Bourgogne*, snails; *les oeufs en meurette*, poached eggs in a wine sauce; *andoulette*, a white sausage; and Bresse poultry. Burgundy is famous for its Charolais cattle, which provide excellent steaks and the makings for *boeuf bourguignon*. Lamb is also superb.

Before your meal try *kir*, a happy combination of black currant liqueur and white wine, and *gougères*, a delicious local puff pastry.

The rivers produce a number of fish specialty dishes including a freshwater *bouillabaisse*, stew. Carp and trout are also worth trying.

Almost every village has its own special cheese, of which the most noteworthy are *époisses* and *St. Florentin*, made from cow's milk, and *banton de culotte*, made from goat's milk. Burgundian desserts include gingerbread, anise-seed pastries, and a bewildering number of dishes made with the fruits of the region.

After-dinner drinks favored in the region include *marc*, the fiery distillation of the skin and pips of grapes after the final pressing, and *fine de Bourgogne*.

Menus will often offer dishes followed by the term: *à la Dijonnaise*. This means with a mustard sauce. The mustard for which Dijon is world famous was originally brought in by the Romans.

Chapter 21

About the Burgundy Canal

T he Canal de Bourgogne, which will be your close companion for 133 miles from Dijon to Migennes, is considered by some the most beautiful route in the entire country. It is also one of the most rugged. Your path takes you past 165 locks and across the highest summit of any on the entire French canal system.

Your canalside journey will wend its serpentine way generally northwestward. It is one of four roughly parallel canal routes linking the basin of the Seine with the basin of the Rhône, and thus the Atlantic, with the Mediterranean. Our route begins at Dijon and will terminate at the village of Migennes, where the canal delivers you at its northern terminus, the River Yonne, a tributary of the Seine.

You will encounter locks about every half-mile between Dijon and the canal summit, at 1,240 feet above sea level. At the outset you will be pedaling alongside the swift River Ouche through a narrowing and steep-sided valley. From Dijon to the summit, about 33 miles, 52 locks were needed. When a mountain finally blocks its way, the canal disappears into a tunnel more than 2 miles long.

The rulers of France as far back as François I in the sixteenth century dreamed of a water route between the English Channel and the Mediterranean. Work actually started in 1606, but was abandoned and restarted several times over the next two centuries due to money problems. It was not until 1832, in the golden age of canal transport, that the first vessel moved through the completed canal. Unfortunately, the canal didn't become fully operational for several more years, just in time to feel competition from other canals traversing the region and, more importantly, from the new age of railroading. The Burgundy Canal never really lived up to the dreams of its promoters, and today commercial barges have virtually disappeared. It is used almost

When cycling along the canals, cyclists will ride through forest and past historic stately homes.

entirely by pleasure boats. Even these are not nearly as numerous as on the Midi or the Brittany canals, however, probably due to the density of locks.

Take courage. While in the world of canal engineering the Burgundy Canal sets a standard for ascents, it is hardly noticeable to the cyclist who still pedals along the level canalside, his pace scarcely slowed by short, sharp, 12- to 15-foot inclines marking the next lock.

Chapter 22

Along the Canal de Bourgogne from Dijon to Pouilly-en-Auxois

Your starting point, Dijon, is the ancient capital of the Dukes of Burgundy. Remains of their splendor live on untarnished by war or conquest, preserved and venerated by their successors. Dijon today is a bustling light industrial and commercial hub, a university center, but even more, a magnificent showcase for its past. It boasts more than 10 museums. Dijon is turrets, gargoyles, half-timber, luxurious flower gardens, rank upon rank of colorful medieval flags. It's also a place where your budget, justifiably, may take a beating. Its wines and gastronomic offerings are world-class seducers.

If you arrive by train (it's only 95 minutes by TGV from Paris), go straight ahead from the station door up the Avenue Foch. Small and inexpensive commercial hotels line Avenue Foch and the side streets. The tourist office is on your left in the second block.

Just beyond the tourist office is the busy Place d'Arcy, one of the ancient gates of the city. More expensive hotels can be found here. By following Rue de la Liberté, the city's principal shopping street, you will come to the charming medieval town, filled with architectural and historic landmarks. Head for the Place François Rude, which you will recognize by its fountain with its heroic statue of a man stomping grapes. Close by is the thirteenth century Church of Notre Dame, loaded with gargoyles and, inside, a mechanical clock dating to 1383.

Dijon is home to the University of Dijon, which is probably responsible for the city's high standing in diverse technical fields. The city's products include pharmaceuticals, instruments, and electronics.

The town has many fine restaurants, mellow *cafés*, shops, museums, palaces, and old mansions—well worth a stopover before beginning your canalside adventure.

To start your canalside journey from Dijon, head for the small boat harbor, the *port du plaisance*, and take the right-hand towpath heading at first, west. Very soon it disappears, forcing you to take to a parallel street, but at the first lock, Larrey (No. 54), you can return. Here the canal takes a sharp right turn and the path has a paved surface.

The first three locks are all within the Dijon metropolis, and you pass a number of high-rise apartment houses and developments, residential and industrial. A new bicycle path, very similar to the *Piste Cyclable* near Toulouse, leads you through the outer suburbs in grandeur. Soon you pass, on your right, Lac Kir, fed by the river Ouche. Here also is a station for the Petit Train de la Côte d'Or, a narrow-gauge railroad that parallels your path for several miles, as does the river.

The upgraded section of the towpath ends at Lock Plombières (No. 50) but the old path is a comfortable ride with only a

---

Suggested Detour

The heart of the Burgundy wine country is a narrow strip of very highly prized real estate about 12 miles long and often no more than a few hundred yards wide, stretching west of the River Saône and south of Dijon along what is called the *Route des Grands Crus*. Before starting off in the opposite direction along the canal path, you might want to loosen up some pumping muscles with a one- or two-day detour through two of the greatest wine-making regions of the world: Côte de Nuit and Côte de Beaune.

From these two neighboring regions, comprising less than 100 square miles, come the wines of 29 *appelations controlées*, legendary names such as Chamertan, St. Denis, Pommard, Montrachet, Les Maranges, and Meursault.

You should leave the city on Avenue Jean-Jaures and follow signs for D 122. About 10 miles south of Dijon, watch for the village of Vougeot. The main attraction is the Château du Clos de Vougeot. It is to wine-making what Wimbledon is to tennis. It is the seat of *the Confrérie des Chevaliers de Tastevin*, perhaps the world's leading authority on wine-making. Stop and visit its historic cellars and view its twelfth century presses.

From Nuits St. George follow D 8 and D 18. Beaune, dominated by picturesque ramparts, is another 10 miles farther on and should be an objective. It is the undisputed center of Burgundy wine-making. When you tire of wine tasting, you might want to visit Hôtel Dieu, a hospital that continues to take care of the sick, 500 years after its founding.

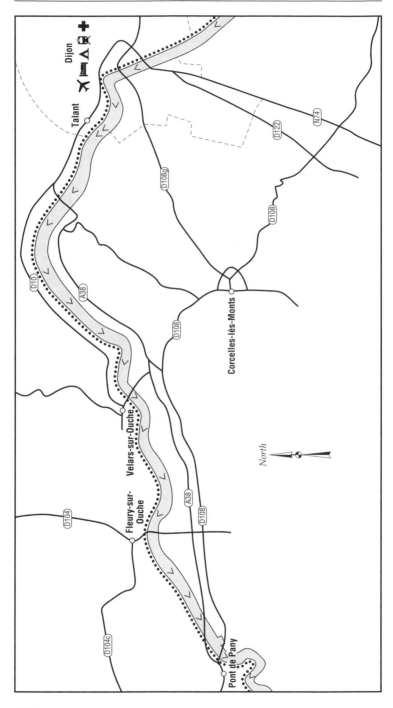

few isolated bumps. A busy superhighway, A 38, keeps company with the river and canal along the floor of the narrow valley.

Locks come up with regularity about every half mile. All are original and manually operated. The gates are opened and closed by means of a long lever. Watch out as you pass by that you don't get skewered.

Your curiosity may be piqued by the only obvious lock improvement, a tiny shed about the size of telephone booth. It is a sign of the times. Until recently each lock had a lockkeeper who lived with his family in the small and simple house next to the locks. Today, with almost no commercial boats, and even scarce pleasure boats, the government saves money by hiring circuit lockkeepers to oversee a number of locks. The little booths shelter the transient lockkeeper while he waits for business.

At Lock Crucifix (No. 47) the walls of the valley close in and get steeper. A crucifix can be seen at the top of a rock pinnacle on your left. At the next lock, a very impressive high railroad bridge spans a tributary valley to the right. Take care; the path surface here is a bit potholed.

At Velars (No. 45) you can visit some mustard factories. A supermarket is close on your right, as is a post office. A restaurant, Auberge Gourmande, is noteworthy. Here the river Ouche runs swift and deep very close on your right, separated from the canal only by the ubiquitous rank of poplar sentinels. How tempting on a hot day! Why not?

At Lock Fleurey (No. 42) the path improves past a school and a couple of attractive restaurants. At Pont de Pany (No. 38) there is a very attractive inn with restaurant, plus a small village with most services.

You don't have to leave the canal bank for provisioning in this neighborhood. Several of the lockkeepers have turned their houses into shops.

Your approach to the summit is obvious as the valley becomes narrower with each mile and the locks become more dense; the hills become steeper, closer, and more wooded, and

---

Author's Note

As you pass by a lock, often someone will come out of the house and look at you questioningly. It is the lockkeeper wondering if you are the advance party for an approaching boat. If there is a boat following you, nod yes. He will start turning valves and opening gates for them. If there isn't a boat close, nod no. He'll resume his nap.

the canal's climb becomes more obvious. But despite the lock density, each one represents barely a 12-foot rise in elevation, hardly noticeable for cyclists.

At Lock Chaume (No. 28) the twentieth century has arrived. The lock has been automated and equipped with stop lights, making lockkeepers redundant. Boatmen control the water level and open the doors themselves.

At Veuvey (No. 22) a small country hotel, Hôtel de la Vallée de l'Ouche, with restaurant and bar, offers a good place to put in for the night. From Veuvey you can easily visit the Côte de Nuit and Côte de Beaune wine-making regions if you missed the detour from Dijon. Take D 115 and D 18 east about 11 miles.

Continuing on, you should cross to the left bank and use D 33, which parallels the canal closely. Rejoin the canal at Pont d'Ouche, a pleasant little place with a boat marina and park. The whole scene here is dominated by a modern curved bridge that carries superhighway A 6 high over the valley. The valley, the river, the canal, and the path take a sharp turn to the right, and it becomes even more obvious that the Canal de Bourgogne is the canal that climbs a mountain.

At Pont d'Ouche you can opt to follow the canal path on the right bank or use D 18, close to the canal on the left. If conditions are wet, use the road and avoid potholes. Between Locks 14 and 13, you can take the bridge serving D 115 to the right a short distance up the hill to a Burgundian gem, Châteauneuf-en-Auxois, with its fifteenth century *château* surrounded by houses of the same era.

Your path is on the left side from Lock Revin (No. 12). At Vandenesse (No. 8) follow the right-hand path. The village of Vandenesse specializes in flower gardens, and a wonderful old castle looks down on it from a hill. There's a general store beside the canal (look down from the lock), and a nest of barges converted for the tourist trade. Some take overnight guests.

You pass seven densely packed locks and arrive at a large turning basin at Escommes. Follow a country lane along the right side of a deep cut to where the canal disappears into a dark and dank hole in the hillside, highly intimidating to novice boatmen. The tunnel, 2 miles long, is a tight fit for boats, and there never was a towpath through it. Instead, barges were initially propelled by bargemen lying on their backs on their cabin tops and pushing with their legs against the tunnel ceiling or with their arms against the walls. More recently, boats were winched through.

A country lane takes you through a wooded glade above the tunnel entrance, where the progress of the canal underneath is marked by two straight lines of trees. Follow the forest road in the

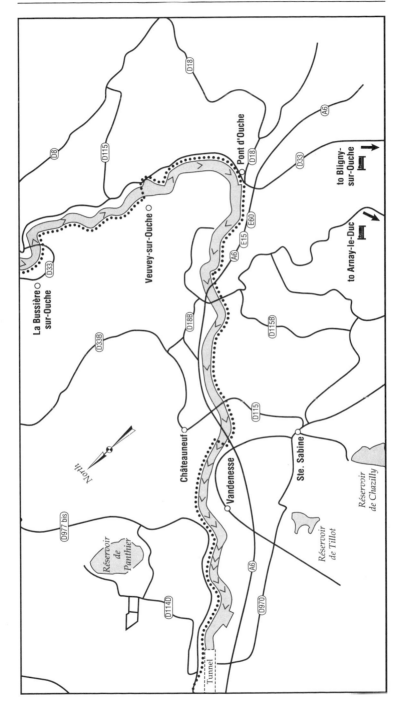

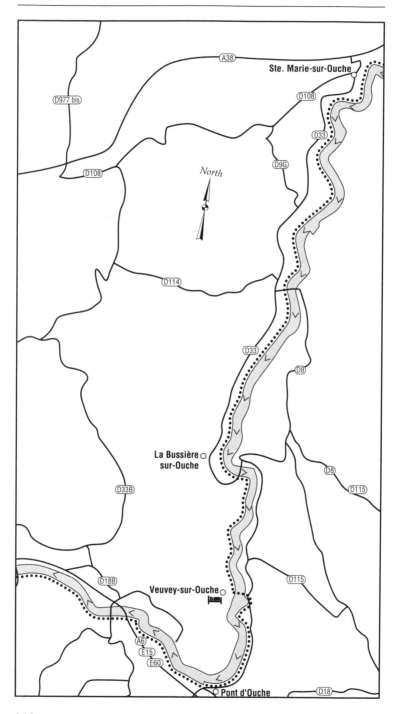

Suggested Detour

From the traffic circle at the canal summit you can visit two three-star Burgundian attractions, Arnay-le-Duc and Autun. At the former is the Maison Regionale, a museum exclusively dedicated to cuisine and the table arts. It is housed in an ancient hospice.

Autun is the ancient capital of the Morvan, Burgundy's hill country, and its history goes back to its founding in 15 B.C. At periods it was the rival of Rome. It was also the headquarters of one of the most famous chefs of all time, Alexandre Dumane.

To visit both towns, follow N 81 southwest from the interchange.

---

same direction on the right and you will pass an old *château* being refurbished. At the summit you come to civilization in the form of a complex traffic rotary, where a number of busy highways intersect. You will find a supermarket, souvenir shops, modern motel, and a number of restaurants catering to transients.

From Pouilly-en-Auxois to Migennes

To resume your itinerary, from the traffic circle take D 18 in the direction of Créancy. You get a good coast to Pouilly-en-Auxois, where the canal emerges from the mountain.

Actually the tunnel passes under most of the town. To find it, take a left oblique from the town center about a block. Pouilly is a modern town with hotels and most services. In the old days it was a major canal port, the place where barges formed into convoys, two per day going each way through the tunnel.

If you have just won the lottery and are looking for grandeur, take the country road that leads west from Pouilly-en-Auxois. About 4 miles from town is the Château Chailly, a recent Japanese acquisition that may be the most exclusive hostelry in the world.

When you rejoin the canal where it emerges from the mountain, take the path on the left bank past another dense lock cluster. You'll note that most of the lockkeepers' houses are derelict. Quite abruptly you leave population behind and emerge into the wide valley of the River Armançon where the only reminder of the twentieth century is the sound of traffic on the Paris-bound Autoroute A 6 on your left. You pass close to the Château d'Eguilly, and in the town are some *chambres d'hôte* in case you are ready to quit for the day. Just beyond Lock Eguilly (No. 11), the path disappears into the tall grass and it doesn't exist on either side for the next few miles. Take the first bridge and a left onto D 970, which parallels the canal close on the right. D 970 is

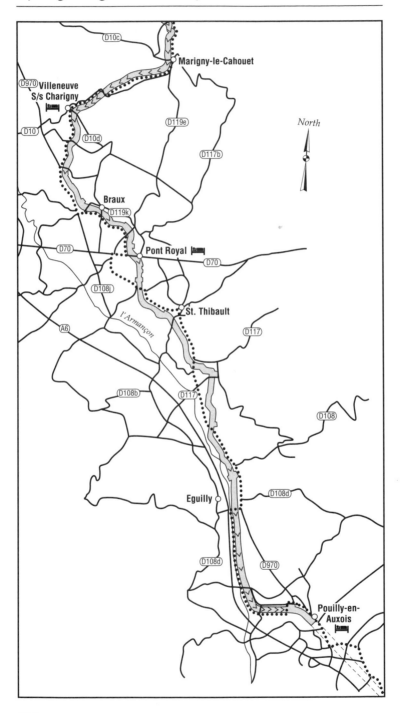

not heavily traveled as it swings back and forth over the waterway. At St. Thibault, stop and admire the thirteenth century church. D 970 leaves the canal for a bit and intersects with D 70. By taking D 70 to the right, you will get back to the canal at a wide place called Pont Royal.

The path recommences on the left. It is no parkway, but the underlying gravel is hard and fairly smooth. Across from the village of Braux the path once more disappears. Take to D 970 again and it takes you directly to Lock Braux (No. 15).

Hotels and even restaurants along this section are rare, but close by is an opportunity for accommodation. At Lock Charigny (No. 16), turn left onto a country road and you will come to a simple but friendly roadside inn, Auberge de Chaudron, quite close to the hamlet of Villeneuve Charigny. From Lock 16, the left-hand path improves markedly for no apparent reason. Within the next 7 miles you will encounter 36 locks. It makes a pleasant downhill run. At Lock 18 you may be welcomed by an expatriate Swiss couple, who make their home in the former lockkeeper's house. At the bridge just beyond Lock 20, change to the right-hand side.

Another Suggested Detour

B etween Locks 45 and 46, take the country road that heads off to the right. Within a few miles you will come to Flavigny-sur-Ozerain, a picturesque little village built on a rock and bordered on three sides by water. It was founded in the eighth century, and many of its currently in-use buildings substantiate it. Try the anise-seed candies, a longtime local specialty.

Rather than return to the canal by the same route, you might want to circle back via Alise-Sainte-Reine. The town, important for its archaeological diggings and museum, was named for a local lady who was beheaded for refusing to marry the Roman governor.

Close by is the Château Bussy-Rabutin built by another local, famous for not going with the flow. Roger Rabutin was a noble and a cartoonist who couldn't bring himself to stop making fun of King Louis XIV and his court. Louis put him in the Bastille for a year, then banished him to his *château,* where flamboyant Roger continued to practice his satire and whimsy undeterred. His motto was: "If others are for it, I'm against." His *château,* open to the public, displays the work of this early individualist. It's a nice downhill ride back into the valley to meet the canal at Venarey-les-Laumes.

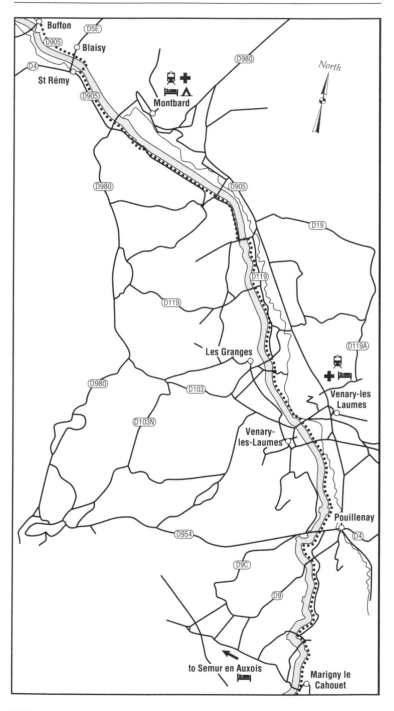

You will find an opportunity for shopping at Lock 26, where the village of Marigny-le-Cahouet offers a number of shops and a good restaurant, The Refuge. From here there is a worthwhile detour to Semur-en-Auxois, about 8 miles to the left of the track. Perched on a pink granite rock, it is a well-preserved medieval market town.

After Lock Venarey (No. 55), take a right to get into the bustling town of Venarey-les-Laumes, which has a rail station, several hotels and supermarkets, and is the capital of the Auxois region. The plain you just passed through, according to local stories, was the site of the Battle of Alésia in 52 B.C., a turning point in Caesar's conquest of Gaul. From Venarey the path continues on the right bank. Across the canal you pass a farm village, Les Granges, with a big smokestack and a tree growing out of its top. As you approach the important town of Montbard, the path is top quality, but at Lock Courcelles (No. 61), cross over and take highway D 119 through the pretty hillside village of Nogent. Rejoin the canal through a picturesque area of big, old homes. Continue on the left bank for the remaining mile or so to Montbard. Perched on the steep side of the valley, Montbard makes an excellent overnight stop, offering a number of good hotels. It is a canal port and a metalworking center, and claims the naturalist Buffon as a native son. Worth visiting are the Fine Arts Museum in the Buffon Institute, the office where he worked, and the Buffon Chapel, where he is buried.

It was in Montbard that the Free French armies, one from Normandy and one from the Mediterranean, met following the allied invasions of World War II. A good cycle shop is on the lower level of the town.

From Montbard it is a 4-mile ride to Fontenay Abbey, a well-maintained example of a Cistercian monastery of the twelfth century. It was founded by Saint Bernard in 1118. Take D 32.

Resuming the canal, take the left side, a well-maintained gravel path, and stay left until you arrive at Lock St. Remy (No. 67). Switch to the right and pass by the fabricator of what looks like huge plastic bottle caps and next door, a picturesque manor house.

After the manor house, take highway D 905 to the village of Buffon, which advertises a hotel and *chambre d'hôte,* and is a tourist center by dint of the historic forge operated there in the eighteenth century by the Buffon family. In its time it was state-of-the-art in metalworking. It has been restored and is open to the public.

At the first bridge beyond the village, cross over to the left side of the canal. For the next 10 miles, to Ancy-le-Franc, your track will traverse some densely wooded countryside dotted with fascinating and picturesque villages. A stop at Cry, Nuits, or Ravières, all close by the canal, is worth the time.

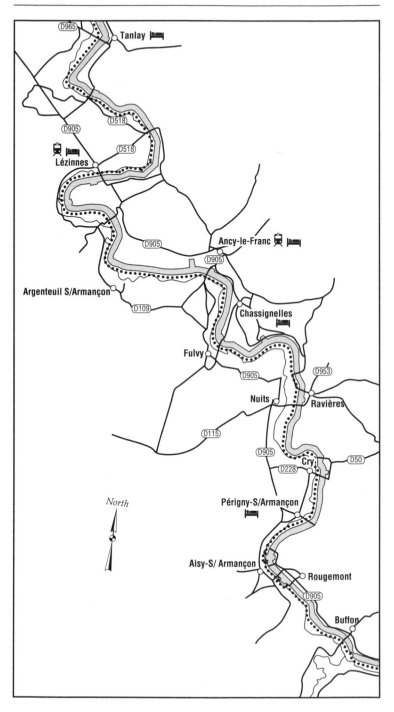

Looking for a laundry? Montbard doesn't have one, but in Cry there's one that needs no coins. It's a historic, covered *laverie* where folks for centuries did it the old-fashioned way. Some still do. Cry, reached by crossing a fifteenth century bridge built on the Armançon, is the first of many towns specializing in granite and marble working. The rock is quarried from the big escarpments you can see on the heights to the east.

At Ravières are still more large marble and granite works, and if you are hungry, try the unprepossessing Chez Daniel, a typical country *café* frequented by the marble workers and local farmers. The food is not fancy, but it is well prepared, inexpensive, and very ample.

Soon after Lock Fulvy (No. 78), your path runs through what remains of a large granite mill that appears to have abruptly gone out of business. Peeking through the shattered windows you can see blueprints and invoices scattered around the office and work in process left as it was the day production stopped.

Ancy-le-Franc is a charming village that beckons tourists with excellent camping facilities, old houses, and in its center probably the most beautiful *château* in Burgundy. This opulent renaissance palace, built in the style of an Italian palazzo, is really four separate but identical wings, joined at the corners by towers. In the stables of the *château* is an interesting auto and harness museum, which includes an 1898 De la Haye.

From Ancy, stay on the left bank, on a good path under the rail bridge. Lock Argenteuil (No. 82) is a very pretty lock. After you pass a number of large grain storage plants, you'll be surprised to find yourself in the middle of a large and active La Farge cement factory. Stay close to the canal bank. Nobody will bother you, but keep out of the way as the huge loading machines speed back and forth.

Tanlay is a most attractive Burgundian market town with a remarkable renaissance *château* in its center. Surrounded by moats, it is an elegant fourteenth century palace. Many of its rooms are open to the public and are filled with magnificent furniture and furnishings.

If you are in the mood for a hamburger and fries, check out the canalside snack bar, Chez Milou, operated by an English couple, Brian and Carolyn Hurst, at the village of Commisey. They are former tourist barge operators as are their friends Jonathan and Trini, who run the Mongolfier, a charming *chambre d'hôte* in nearby St. Martin-sur-Armançon.

The path from Commissey to Tonnerre continues on the left bank, and is part of a mountain bike course for a cycling club based in Tonnerre. It is in excellent condition. At Tonnerre, check out Vieil Hôpital, which was founded in 1293 by

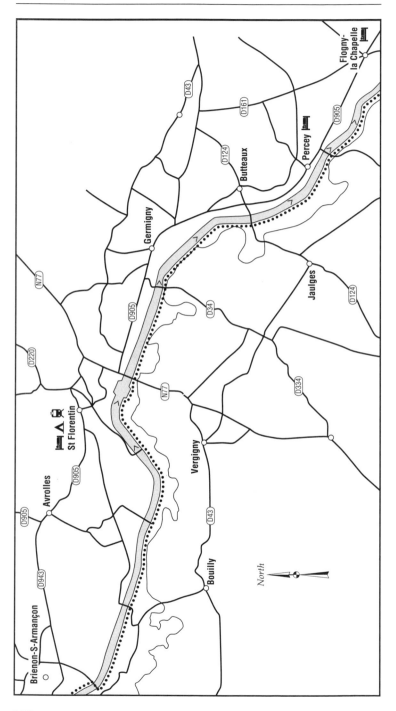

Marguerite de Bourgogne and is 150 years older than the more famous Hôtel Dieu in Beaune. This great grandfather of all hospitals is being restored.

Close to the canal and the swift-running Armançon is a large and attractive camping area with showers and other services. Before leaving Tonnerre, walk through the old town, and don't miss the *Fosse Dionne*, where the ladies did their washing

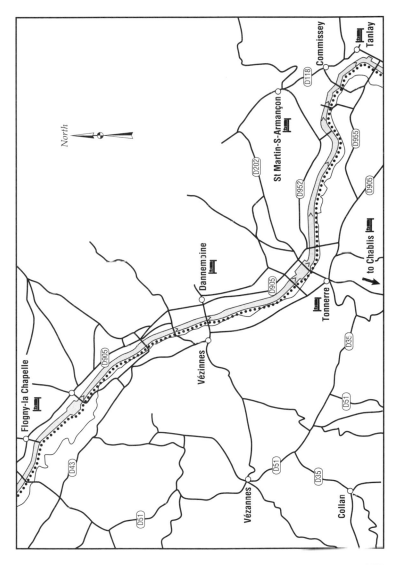

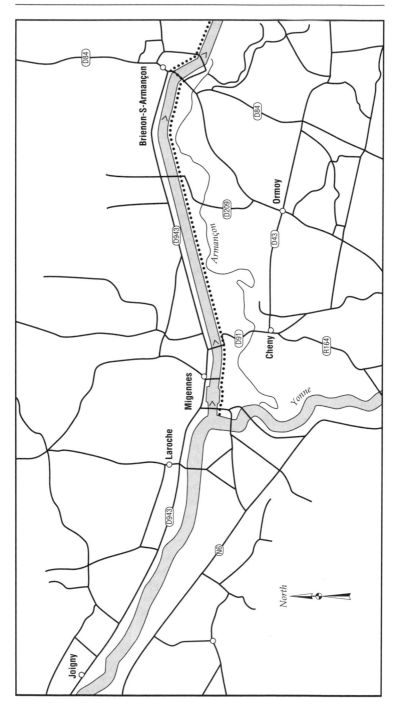

through the centuries, aided by the waters of a bubbling spring. A nasty serpent named Basilic is said to inhabit its depths. From Tonnerre you are only 10 miles from the center of the Chablis wine region. Take N 965 if you are thirsty for some of the best dry, white wine in the world.

Gradually you and the canal emerge from remote ruralness to suburbia. The towns are much closer together now and the homes and farms have changed from rustic to up-market. The path, too, changes. In some places it becomes almost perfect, only to be followed by sections that haven't been touched in years. All in all, however, the path is good and your surroundings most pleasant as you dip close to the River Armançon, which will continue to entice you. Route N 77 crosses your path just before you arrive at the old and picturesque town of St. Florentin. A detour 6 miles down that road will bring you to Pontigny Abbey, founded in 1114. Main line rail service is available in St. Florentin.

Near a huge telephone pole factory is the headquarters of a rental boat firm on the yacht basin serving St. Florentin. If your bike needs servicing, you're in luck; just ahead of the basin along N 77, between the town and the rail station, is a large shop that sells and services bikes and motor bikes. St. Florentin is a good stopping place. In addition to the canal, it is lapped by two rivers, the Armançon and the Armance. Its fourteenth century church has exquisite stained glass of the Troyennes school. Check out the local cheeses, *soumaintrain* and *St. Florentin.*

Ride to Lock Bouloir (No. 111) along the left bank, but there take a short detour on the right to the next bridge. This gets you around a petro-chemical plant. Cross back to the left for the rest of your journey, about 6 miles to the canal's end. There is a magnificent old oval washing place in the town of Brienon, along with good shops and a thirteenth century church.

Laroche-Migennes is definitely a part of the twentieth century. It is a major rail center with huge marshaling yards, where in former days all trains had to stop to change engines before entering or leaving the Paris area. For us it is the end of the line. The canal ends at the River Yonne, a tributary of the Seine. To continue the remaining 80 miles to Paris by bike, it's necessary to mix with traffic and navigate by public highway. To go by train (in less than an hour) you will find the rail station close to the canal. Service is frequent. There are a number of attractive hotels and restaurants near the station.

Chapter 23

Canal de Bourgogne—Accommodations

Hotels, Guest Houses, Campgrounds, Phone Numbers, and Other Useful Information
Note: Communities are listed in order geographically from Dijon toward Migennes at the north end of the canal. Numbers following hotel and guest house listings indicate number of rooms; those following campground listings indicate number of campsites. Number following community name is ZIP code. Stars are the government luxury rating system of France.

Dijon 21000 (Market: Friday, Saturday, Tuesday)
Dijon is the ancient capital of the dukes of Burgundy, a city of medieval antiquity and museums with scores of hotels and points of interest to choose from. For a complete list, contact the Dijon Tourist Office, Place Darcy, 21000 Dijon, Tel. 80 44 11 44; fax 80 42 18 83.

Camping		
Centre de Rencontres		
Internationale	280	80 72 95 20

Pont de Pany 21360
Hotels		
Pont de Pany**		80 23 60 59
Château la Chassagne		80 40 47 50

Veuvey-sur-Ouche 21360
Hotel		
de la Vallée de l'Ouche		80 33 04 39

Bligny-sur-Ouche 21360
Hotels		
Auberge du Val d'Ouche	25	80 20 12 06
Hôtellerie des 3 Faisans		80 20 10 14
Guest Houses		
Château d'Ecutigny		80 20 19 14
le Château	6	80 20 19 14

Marguerite Lioret	3	80 20 12 90
Tourist Office		80 20 16 51

Vandenesse-en-Auxois
Guest House

Barge "Lady"	3	80 49 26 96

Arnay le Duc 21230
Hotels

Chez Camille***	11	80 90 01 38
Chez Henri**		80 90 14 93
Terminus**	9	80 90 00 33
du Daphine	8	80 90 14 25
de la Poste**	14	80 90 00 76

Guest Houses

André et Simone Picard	3	80 90 06 08
René et Michelle Rabian	2	80 90 01 83
Gerald et Veronique Paillard	3	80 84 26 39
Ferme de Lascivia Dracy-Chalas	2	80 90 23 51
l'Arletoise	2	80 90 16 61
Tourist Office		80 90 07 55

Pouilly-en-Auxois 21320
Hotels

Château de Sainte-Sabine***		80 49 22 01
de la Poste		80 90 86 44
du Commerce**	19	80 90 88 23
du Val Vert		80 90 82 34

Guest Houses

la Chouannerie	2	80 33 43 02
la Rente d'Equilly	3	80 90 83 48
Cercey	2	80 90 88 48
Bernard et Madeleine Moreau	2	80 64 61 91
Tourist Office		80 90 74 24

Pont Royal 21390
Guest House

la Maison du Canal		80 90 50 70

Villeneuve-sours-Charigny
Hotel

l'Auberge du Chaudron**	12	80 97 34 10

Flavigny-sur-Ozerain 21150
Hotel

Auberge du Bon Coin		80 96 21 05

Guest Houses

La Grange	7	80 96 01 88
Couvent des Castafours	2	80 96 24 92
Tourist Office		80 96 24 65

Semur-en-Auxois 21140

Hotels

des Négociants*		80 21 14 06
de la Cìté d'Or**		80 97 03 13
des Gourmets*		80 97 09 41
Hôtellerie d'Aussois		80 97 28 28
le Castel**		80 20 45 07
les Cymaises**	11	80 97 21 44
du Lac**	22	80 97 11 11

Guest Houses

Daniel et Françoise Giroudeau	4	80 64 53 86
Bernard et Claudine Virely	2	80 96 44 66
le Château	2	80 97 17 07
Monique et Bernard Dubois	2	80 96 00 47
Youth Hostel		80 97 10 22
Tourist Office		80 97 05 96

Venarey-les-Laumes 21150

Hotels

Alésia		80 96 19 67
Auberge du Château		80 96 17 69

Guest Houses

Dominique Bertrand	1	80 96 22 89
Claude et Huguette Gounand	2	80 96 23 20
Monique Laffage	2	80 96 01 88
Robert et Irene Renardet	2	80 96 01 25
Hospital		80 96 04 84
Tourist Office		80 96 89 13

Montbard 21500

Hotels

Château de Malaisy***		80 89 46 54
de l'Ecu***		80 92 11 66
la Renaissance**		80 92 12 80
le Buffon		80 92 14 70
le Voltaire		80 89 42 21
de la Gare**	34	80 92 02 12

Guest Houses

Sarah Busson	5	80 92 46 00
Odile Balp	3	80 92 44 16
L'Enclos	4	80 92 16 12

Camping		
Municipal****	80	80 92 12 60
Tourist Office		80 92 03 75
Hospital		80 92 02 78

Aisy-sur-Armançon 89390
Hotel
de Bourgogne		86 55 76 46

Chassignelles
Hotel
de l'Ecluse 79	8	86 75 18 51

Ancy-le-Franc 89160 (Market: Thursday)
Hotels
Hôtellerie du Centre**	18	86 75 15 11
de la Poste	6	86 75 11 08
de l'Ecluse	5	86 75 02 04
Tourist Office		86 75 03 15

Lezinnes 89160
Hotel
de la Gare*		86 75 66 14

Tanlay
Hotel
Auberge du Cheval Blanc**		86 75 81 79

St. Martin-sur-Armançon 89700
Guest House
Montgolfier	86 75 81 79

Tonnerre 89700
(Market: Wednesday and Saturday morning)
Hotels
l'Abbaye Saint-Michel****	14	86 55 05 99
de la Fosse Dionne**	12	86 55 11 92
Ibis**	40	86 54 41 41
du Centre	16	86 55 10 56
Guest Houses		
Paul et Monique Batreau	3	86 75 22 76
les Musseaux	1	86 75 24 03
Bertrand Kuzio et François Nathalie	4	86 55 59 02
Daniel et Eliane Copin-Raoult	3	86 55 14 05
Tourist Office		86 55 14 48

Chablis 89800
Hotels
Hôtellerie des Clos***	26	86 42 10 63

de l'Etoile**	14	86 42 10 50
Ibis**	38	86 42 49 20
Guest Houses		
Gilles et Elisabeth Lecolle	3	86 55 26 44
Christian et Nicole Adine	3	86 41 40 28
le Moulin	5	86 75 92 46
Philippe et Magda Garnier	1	86 47 75 15

Collan 89700

Guest House		
la Marmotte	3	86 55 26 44

Dannemoine 81700

Guest House		
la Bichonnière	4	86 55 59 02

Flogny-la-Chapelle 89360

Hotel		
de la Poste	40	86 75 49 20

Percey 89360

Guest House		
M. et Mme Willems	2	86 43 22 32

St. Florentin 89600
(Market: Monday and Saturday morning)

Hotels		
la Grande Chaumière***	10	86 35 15 12
de l'Est**	23	86 35 10 35
les Tilleuls**	9	86 35 09 09
le Moulin des Pommerats***	20	86 35 08 04
la Cruchade*		86 35 02 36
Vieille France		86 35 14 70
Guest House		
René et Marie		
France Debreuve	1	86 36 09 91
Camping		
de l'Armançon**		86 35 08 13
Tourist Office		86 35 11 86

Migennes 89400

Hotels		
de Paris **	10	86 80 23 22
aux Rives de l'Yonne	8	86 80 05 70
l'Escale	12	86 80 20 99
Guest Houses		
Paul et Simone Poncet	3	86 91 94 52
Maud Dufayet	1	86 91 93 48

Appendices

Appendix A—Bibliography

These books might be helpful to anyone considering wandering the French water roads.

Bikes and Traveling
The Bicycle Touring Book, by Tim and Glenda Wilhelm
Living on Two Wheels, by Dennis Coello
France by Train, by Simon Vickers
France by Bike, by Karen and Terry Whitehall
Great Vacations with Kids, by Dorothy Jordan and Marjorie Cohen
Cycling France, by Jerry H. Simpson Jr.
Inland Waterways of France, by David Edwards-May
Traveling with Children and Enjoying It, by Arlene K. Nutter
Through the French Canals, by Philip Bristow
Bicyclists Source Book, the Ultimate Directory of Cycling Information
Paris, by John Russell
A Little Tour of France, by Henry James
Insiders Guide to Air Courier Bargains, by Kelly Monaghan
Travels in Burgundy, by Mary Edsy with Jill Norman
Discovering the Villages of France, by Michael Busselle

Architecture
Form, Function and Design, by Paul Jacques Grillo
Master Builders of the Middle Ages, by David Jacobs
Impressionism, by Jean Leymarie
The Impressionists at First Hand, edited by Bernard Denuir
The Châteaux of France, by Daniel Wheeler

Cuisine
The Foods of France, by Waverly Root
Wines of France, by Alexis Lichine
Eating and Drinking in France Today, by Pamela Vandyke-Price
Burgundy—A Comprehensive Guide to the Producers, Appellations and Wines, by Robert M. Parker Jr.
The Taste of France: Burgundy, by Robert Freson

History
The Birth of France: Warriors, Bishops and Long-Haired Kings, by Katharine
    Scherman
Fleur de Lys—The Kings of France, by Joy Law
The Splendid Century, by W. H. Lewis
The Sun King: Louis XIV, by Nancy Mitford

Appendix B—Conversions

English-French Equivalents
Days of the Week

Monday	lundi	lun dee
Tuesday	mardi	mar dee
Wednesday	mercredi	mare kreh dee
Thursday	jeudi	joo dee
Friday	vendredi	vahn dreh dee
Saturday	samedi	sahm dee
Sunday	dimanche	dee mahnsh

Months of the Year

January	janvier	jahn vee ay
February	février	fave ree ay
March	mars	mars
April	avril	ah vreel
May	mai	my
June	juin	jou ahn
July	juillet	jwee ay
August	août	ah oot
September	septembre	sept ahm breh
October	octobre	oct oh breh
November	novembre	nov ahm breh
December	décembre	day sahm breh

Numbering System

1	un, une	uh, un
2	deux	dew
3	trois	twah
4	quatre	kaht
5	cinq	sank
6	six	seese
7	sept	set
8	huit	wheet
9	neuf	newf
10	dix	deese
11	onze	ohnz
12	douze	dooz
13	treize	trehz
14	quatorze	kah torz

15	quinze	canz
16	seize	sehz
17	dix-sept	dee set
18	dix-huit	dees wheet
19	dix-neuf	dees newf
20	vingt	vahn
21	vingt-et-un	vahn tay uh
30	trente	trahnt
40	quarante	kar ahnt
50	cinquante	sank ahnt
60	soixante	swahz ahnt
70	soixante-dix	swahz ahnt deese
80	quatre-vingt	kaht reh vahn
90	quatre-vingt dix	kaht reh vahn deese
100	cent	sahn
1000	mille	meel

Some Decimal Equivalents

1 kilometre ....62 mile	1 meter ....3.28 feet
5 kilometres...............3.11 miles	5 meters ....16.4 feet
10 kilometres ....6.21 miles	10 meters ....32.8 feet

1 centimeter ....39 inches	1 kilo...............2.2 pounds
5 centimeters............1.95 inches	5 kilos.............11 pounds
10 centimeters..........3.9 inches	10 kilos...........22 pounds

1 litre.........1.05 quarts	0 degrees Celsius......32 degrees Fahrenheit
5 litres.......5.3 quarts	20 degrees Celsius....68 degrees Fahrenheit
10 litres.....10.5 quarts	40 degrees Celsius....104 degrees Fahrenheit

Appendix C—Bicycle Rental Shops

Paris

La Maison du Velo
11, Rue Fenelon
75010 Paris
42 81 24 72

Item Cycle
85, Rue Bobillot
Paris
45 89 40 14

La Boutique du Cycle
6, Rue Emile Gilbert
75012 Paris
43 41 18 10

Paris Velo
2/4 Rue du Fer à Moulin
75005 Paris
43 37 59 22

Rando Cycles
5, Rue Fernand Foureau
75012 Paris
45 00 18 20

Paris by Cycle
99, Rue de la Jonquière
75007 Paris
43 63 36 63

Paris Environs

Maison de Velo Motobécane
Faubourg Chartrain
41100 Vendôme

Cycles Raymond
rue Madeleine E4 Rue Carnot
Versailles

M. Claude LeBlond
44, Levee des Tuileries
41000 Blois

Brittany Region
Nantes

Cybreta Matignon
72, Boulevard Ernest Dalby
Nantes
40 74 05 05

Rennes

Cycles Geffrault
68, Boulevard de Verdon
Rennes
99 59 46 80

Midi Region
Carcassonne

Ets. M. Raynaud
31, Boulevard de Varsovie
11000 Carcassonne
68 25 19 27

14, Rue Jean Monnet
11000 Carcassonne
68 71 67 06

Montirat (near Carcassonne)

M. Gerard de Castro, Le Joug
11800 Montirat
68 78 73 78

Toulouse

La Boutique du Cycle
64, fg Bonnefoy
Toulouse
61 48 37 11

Montaubin

Cycles Guionnet
51, Boulevard Alsace Lorraine
Montaubin
63 63 58 02

Burgundy Region
Dijon

La Ferme Creuse
3, Rue de Beaune
Dijon
80 55 54 65

Cycles Dutrion
29, Rue Pasteur
Dijon
80 66 54 50

Travel Bike Location
28, Boulevard de la Marne
Dijon
80 72 31 00

Cycles Theurel
81, Rue Berbisey
Dijon
80 30 86 80

Sens

Cycles Villebenoit
rue Gal Leclerc
Sens
86 64 48 97

St. Jean de Losne

Fabien Thevenot
21170 St. Jean de Losne
80 39 20 79

Appendix D—Air Courier Firms

The following companies sometimes provide discounted air tickets in exchange for air courier services:

Courier Travel Service
529 Central Avenue
Cedarhurst, NY 11516
800-922-8279

Now Voyager
74 Varick Street
New York, NY 10013

Halbart Express
147-05 176th Street
Jamaica, NY 11434
718-656-8279

World Courier, Inc.
137-42 Guy R. Brewer Blvd.
Jamaica, NY 11434
800-221-6600

Appendix E—Bike Carrying Cases and Bags

Following is a partial list of manufacturers of hard- and soft-sided, reusable transport cases and bags:

Pedal Pack Inc.
P.O. Box 788
Porterville, CA 93258
800-359-3096
Hard, fitted cases of polyethylene plastic for two-wheelers, tandems, and two bikes.

Tricosports Inc.
13541 Desmond St.
Pacoima, CA 91331
800-473-7705
Hard-sided shell case with internal foam. Fits all road and mountain bikes. Lockable.

Tandem Two's Day
Green Glen Cycling
4065 W. 11th Ave.
Eugene, OR
800-777-0258
Manufacturer's folding travel system, which includes Samsonite

case to fit their own high-performance, custom tandems. Can convert to two-wheel trailer. Also soft case.

Montague USA
Cambridge, MA
800-736-5348
Hard-sided case principally for the company's own "bicycles that fold" line. Accessory converts case to one-wheel trailer. For tandems, too.

Sac-O-Velo
Cycle Pop
978 Rachel E.
Montreal, Quebec H2J 2J3
Canada
514-524-7102
Soft cases made from 630-denier nylon with interior pockets for dismantled wheels. Additional space for other goodies. Also double-wide case for two bikes. Tandems, too.

Bike Pro USA
3701 W. Roanoke
Phoenix, AZ 85009-1325
800-338-7581
Lightweight, hard-shell case without rigid bottom. Interior padding. Designed to fit airport lockers.

Automaxi
1315 W. Belmont
Chicago, IL 60657-3208
800-345-8677
Hard, polyethylene case designed for both hand carrying and car roof mounting.

Performance
P.O. Box 2741
Chapel Hill, NC 27514
800-727-2453
Tough, rigid case with good interior packing and divider.

Tri-All 3 Sports
927 Calle Negocio, Suite O
San Clemente, CA 92673
800-733-7231
Velo-safe, lockable, rolling hard case made from ABS plastic. Models to accommodate one or two bikes.

Index